LAURA GRISI

A Selection of Works
with Notes by the Artist

Essay-Interview by
Germano Celant

RIZZOLI
NEW YORK

First published in the United States of America in 1990
by Rizzoli International Publications, Inc.
300 Park Avenue South, New York, NY 10010

Library of Congress Cataloging-in-Publication Data
Grisi, Laura.
Laura Grisi/essay-interview by Germano Celant.
Includes bibliographical references.
1. Grisi, Laura—Interviews.   2. Artists—Italy—Interviews.
I. Celant, Germano.   II. Title.
N6923.G73A35   1990   89-43706
709' .2—dc20
ISBN: 0-8478-1222-7

Consultant Dan Friedman
Translated from the Italian by Marguerite Shore
Edited by David Frankel

Designed by Massimo Vignelli

Set in type by Trufont Typographers, Inc., Hicksville, New York
Printed by Dai Nippon Printing Company, Japan

Preceding pages: Reflectivity (details), 1977

Contents

Preceding pages:
Racing Car Room *(detail), 1967*

Germano Celant: The artist is a person who works both from his or her own inner depths and as a part of a social and cultural humus. At first, artists develop by following their own egos; at first, they have to convince themselves of the need for exterior, public affirmation. Their awareness of this conflict between interior and exterior leads them to interweave periods of personal consciousness and periods of contextual influence in the different phases of their work. The problem of identity begins to make itself felt in the fact that their existence as artists gives rise to works of art, to goods, in which it is possible to recognize a symbolic power or a communicative trace that differs from the content of other goods in the marketplace, for it goes back to an authentic feeling. This feeling can take on the force of an unusual event or of a different experience, small or large, it doesn't matter. Thus the artistic personality arises out of a deep uneasiness, for it is tied both to interior processes and to, for example, personal relationships established with other intellectuals, or to the reading of their work. These are the first mechanisms to transform a person into an artist. Can you tell me about your beginnings as an artist, about the cultural soil out of which you grew?

Laura Grisi: I began working in a continuous way between 1964 and 1965. Before that, during what I suppose you would call my formative years, I read a lot, and tried to condense abstract sensations into images. It was then that I went to art school in Rome, and also studied drawing, at the Accademia, and etching and engraving in a private studio on the via Babuino. My friend Domenico Gnoli had introduced me to the studio, where he too was making etchings. We often visited museums together, or went to the Palatine to see the frescoes in the house of the Empress Giulia. Or else we searched out unknown ancient fountains or Baroque carved doorways in the old town. When Gnoli went to New York, he wrote me a letter of his impressions while the boat was coming into New York Harbor. When I opened the letter, a blue butterfly sprang out and flew up into the room; it eventually fell to the ground, and I realized that it was made of paper with a small rubber band attached, which had remained compressed in the sealed envelope, but suddenly unwound when I opened the letter, making the butterfly seem to fly.

In that period, I often went to buy books from a bookseller near the Trevi Fountain. He specialized in things that you couldn't find in other bookstores—out-of-print editions and antique books. There I found Guillaume Apollinaire's *Les Peintres Cubistes,* and some very small leather-bound volumes, printed in the 19th century, of works by Virgil and Plato, as well as *La Vita Nuova* by Dante. This latter work is now in

10

one of my pieces, the wall sculpture *Apollinaire's Secret*. Resting on a plaster shelf, it can be taken out and read, while an identical book, cast in bronze, remains on the shelf. At the same bookseller's I also found another rare book, *La Femme 100 Têtes* by Max Ernst, with his engravings telling the story of LopLop and other characters. Later that book was stolen.

GC: They say that the artist lives in a world of things and images, a forest of signs that are revealed to the glance and thus become known and evident. Yet the corporeality of these sensations grows out of primary realizations almost from adolescence, when one moves about blindly, looking for the path that will become one's life's voyage. At first, the things one sees emerge from one's familiar surroundings. Later on, one ventures on more personal wanderings, searching out buried and hidden moments. In your work I sense that an entire system of images is sanctioned by a constant movement, to the point where your early works, dated 1965–66, are "variable," that is, they move and slide before the eye of the observer, creating superimpositions and intersections of images and sensations. In addition, many of the figures that enter your iconography reveal what seems like the exotic, sometimes oriental qualities and simple truths of primitive myths. They are often aggregates of a fine dusting of color that forms a desertlike powder, and that contains the memory of voyages and events from both childhood and maturity. Can you talk about the planet of images in which you have moved?

LG: I want to describe the cultural and family context of my childhood. What my father liked best was reading and doing research in physics, mathematics, and geometry. He also studied and carried out experiments with radio and with magnetic fields. This wasn't his real work, but it was what interested him most. Two of his projects—one for the remote control of objects by radio, another dealing with the electrical energy produced through an exchange of magnetic waves—were analyzed by a group of American technicians. They found his work so interesting that they invited him to work with them at the Massachusetts Institute of Technology in Cambridge, but he preferred to continue his experiments on his own. I used to talk to him about geometry, logic, gravity, relativity, and everything else I wanted to know in those fields, and he gave me books by Bertrand Russell, Albert Einstein, Henri Bergson, and others.

My father had a film production and distribution company. One of his films won first prize at the Venice Film Festival. He was also very interested in automobiles; he bought one of the first Cisitalias, a beautifully designed car, famous in the '50s, and now exhibited at The Museum of Modern Art in New York. His work brought him into contact with many directors and writers: he knew Alessandro Blasetti, Roberto Rossellini, Augusto Genina (with whom he made two films), Leonide Moguy, Vitaliano Brancati, and Giuseppe Berto. This was the climate and the context in which my brother Fausto and I grew up; he too is involved with film—he has made three, and now has a film and advertising company in Venezuela. In fact, I seem to be the only one in my family who is not a professional filmmaker. As it turned out, my son Brando started his own film production company right after high school, writing and directing his own series of films for television.

My mother was Italian, but was born in Istanbul. She knew six languages well, and almost always spoke French to us at home. She used to paint watercolors, using images of the Turkish landscape, views of Istanbul, and colorful street scenes. She played the piano very well, especially music by Liszt and Mozart, and she also used to sing classical songs. She had a wonderful voice. She often told us about her childhood in Turkey; her father, my grandfather, had owned construction companies and had built, among other things, a harbor on the Bosphorus and roads in Anatolia. When he visited projects in the Turkish interior, my grandmother always wanted to go with him; she loved travel and adventure. They went by horse, followed by an escort, because the countryside was dangerous, wild and full of gangs of thieves. Then my mother would describe the old city, the souks and mosques, and she would tell me about the Turkish women who at the time never went out on the streets, but had arcaded corridors from one house to another, so they could move about without being seen from the outside. Then there was a great rebellion, and foreigners had to leave the country; my grandparents' villa was burned down, and they managed to flee to Rhodes, in Greece (where I was later born). My mother gave me records and books of French poetry—Charles Baudelaire, Arthur Rimbaud, Paul Verlaine, Paul Éluard, Paul Valéry.

GC: Amid the maps and the itineraries covered, there is your own city, and the whole world of education and school. Then the places one visits become a form of knowledge; one's encounters with people from foreign countries and cultures come to seem sometimes curious, sometimes different, and what is different offers a crucial perspective on one's familiar environment. To what artistic realities do you owe your formation?

LG: I attended the art school in Rome and then took classes on and off at the École des Beaux Arts in

Paris. We were in that city because my father was producing a film with French partners. When my family returned to Rome, I stayed on in Paris for the entire season, and the people I met and the books I read there were far more important to me than my academic studies. I got to know students and writers and poets at the Galerie du Dragon, and at Matta's house, in Saint-Germain-des Prés, I met Alain Jouffroy and Jean Jacques Lebel, a writer and poet who had known André Breton and Tristan Tzara. I had just finished reading Breton's *Nadja* and the writings of Antonin Artaud. Lebel and I talked often about Surrealist art and literature; I wanted to know more about the "poem objects" and the "exquisite corpse" games, and he knew many anecdotes and interesting stories about that period. One day we went to the Reine Blanche, the café where Breton used to meet with his group in the days of Surrealism. But the Surrealist world was of only relative interest to me. The primitive art that I saw at Lebel's house (his father, Robert Lebel, had a beautiful collection) also seemed interesting, but so distant from me. Later, traveling in Africa and Polynesia, I felt a real love for primitive and ritual objects, and I too began to collect them.

GC: To lose oneself in one's early experiences is a fantastic thing: through memory, one can see how certain events and moments have had important formative consequences. The effects of such moments cannot be diminished; they force one to reinterpret what one already knows about oneself. Now it seems to me that your work, from the beginning, has presented a certain "theatricality," connected to its often large scale and to its awareness of the fictitious illusion of the spectacle. Even if you have made real voyages throughout the world, the places discovered by your works are more like expeditions into the artificial, into fiction, as if into the industrial culture of reproduction and repetition. They pertain to territories unknown to the human eye, but tied rather to the technological and mediated glance. Where does this fascination with fiction and with the labyrinth of artificial images come from?

LG: A lot of it comes from my reading and from my early experiences with art and with the theater. My favorite artist when I was growing up was Jackson Pollock; though I had seen only one actual painting, I knew his work well in reproduction. I also liked Wols, and, especially, Constantin Brancusi. I was interested in photography, and took a lot of photographs that I developed and printed myself. I read a lot—I particularly remember Jean-Paul Sartre, André Gide, Goethe, Voltaire, Marcel Proust, the Comte de Lautréamont, and Thomas Mann—and I liked plays, because of the structure of the dialogue. I'm thinking

of Miguel de Unamuno, Samuel Beckett, Alfred Jarry, and Bertolt Brecht. Then, in Paris, I got to know two Russian set and costume designers, the Doboujinskis, a couple who has been in the theater world forever. They had an atelier near Montmartre where ten people worked, all Russians, and at the time they were making sets and costumes for Jean Baptiste Lully's *Armide*. They were making plaster casts from which they could model large masks to be part of the costumes. I immediately offered to help, and I worked with them for three months, during which I learned a great deal about Russian culture, from music to theater, from poetry to painting, from Stanislavsky to Sergei Eisenstein, from Sergei Prokofiev to El Lissitzky and Vladimir Mayakovsky. It all seemed to come alive, because when they were young they had worked with Stanislavsky, they had known Mayakovsky, and their stories were fascinating. I wasn't even 18 yet, and it all seemed so extraordinary to me. We went together to the movies to see Eisenstein's films—*Que Viva Mexico* and *The Battleship Potemkin*. I also remember Jacques Feyder's *La Kermesse Héroïque*.

One thing that was very important for me at the Doboujinskis' was the immediate contact with pictorial techniques and with materials. In their atelier, everyone was always "inventing" materials to make objects that, on the set, had to seem completely real, but that were really composed of so-called "fake" stuff. We had to manipulate the "fiction" of the stage, for example, by using a plastic that would seem transparent and light under the theater lights, or a tulle or silk, maybe chosen only for its color, that could be rigidified with a special glue that they knew how to prepare, and that then would seem like a polished metal surface. All this was useful to me later. My "Neon Paintings," 1966–67, for example, were made out of many different materials, from metal and wood to fabric and rubber; and the neon lights created the appearance of a depth that was actually nonexistent, because they were seen through the refraction of a Plexiglas veil, transparent but ribbed, which I twisted on the diagonal.

GC: Your early interest in art dates from the beginning of the '60s, when the climate in Rome and Milan favored finding a way out of *art informel* and American action painting. I remember well the artistic scene in Rome around the Piazza di Spagna and the situation defined by the Tartaruga gallery, which showed the work of Franz Kline, Mark Rothko, and Cy Twombly, as well as young artists like Jannis Kounellis, Mario Schifano, Franco Angeli, and Tano Festa. There was a clear focus on popular icons, and on the theme of the city as a system of sign structures. But I must point out that while Schifano and Kounellis integrated objective data, in the form of street signs or advertising, immediately into their work, your discourse turned more in the direction of a self-reflexive image, as if the subjective had to prevail over the industrial objectuality. In fact, your "Variable Paintings," 1965–66, include your profile, or I should say your shadow, interlaced in an almost metaphysical manner with details that would have been appreciated by Giorgio de Chirico, like the square rule, the arc, the target, and the circle. But what was the artistic situation in which you found yourself when you began your visual journey?

LG: When I got back to Rome from Paris, I began to frequent galleries like the Tartaruga, the Marlborough, and the Attico, and I met many artists there. I also went to Milan, where I knew Piero Manzoni, Vincenzo Agnetti, Gastone Novelli, and Lucio Fontana. I had painted two small works in enamel on canvas, and Fontana looked at them and bought them. (He often bought work from young artists.) When I had my first show in Milan, in 1965, he came to see it. I visited his studio and he gave me a gouache, an oval with holes.

In Rome, at the Tartaruga gallery, I saw a show of Twombly's work that impressed me. Marlborough was showing the work of Toti Scialoja, Achille Perilli, Piero Dorazio, Carla Accardi, Giulio Turcato, and the sculptor Nino Franchina. I knew these artists well, and saw them often at the Herlitzkas' house, or at Rosati's in the Piazza del Popolo. Franchina's wife, Gina, was also there often; she was the daughter of Gino Severini. All this went on, however, for only a short period, because I stayed in Rome just a few months. During that period, I had met Folco Quilici, the film director and writer who had made *Blue Continent* and *Last Paradise*; and just a month later we were married and left for South America, where he was shooting a film in the Andes. From that time on I traveled for long periods with him, which was an extraordinary experience. Because of the type of films he made, we were always looking for places where tribal cultures still existed, to document the last traces of cultures, practices, customs, and rituals that were disappearing.

This is how I came into contact with so many peoples and cultures that were distant from my own cultural context, an experience that strongly influenced my way of thinking and of visualizing life. During those years I read Claude Lévi-Strauss, James Joyce, Robert Musil, Dylan Thomas, and Pier Paolo Pasolini. I discovered Jorge Luis Borges while I was living for some months in Buenos Aires, and he impressed me deeply. While I was traveling, I could only make easily portable pieces like gouaches and drawings, and

so I concentrated on photography and writing. I published a photographic book, *Pasos por Buenos Aires*, and during a year when we were in Polynesia, I wrote another book, *I Denti del tigre*, set on the atolls of Tuamotu.

After a year I spent traveling between the Andes, the pampas, Bolivia, Terra di Missiones, and Buenos Aires, my son, Brando Quilici, was born in Buenos Aires. We spent another year in Polynesia, and many months in Africa, and then returned to Rome, where I started my first paintings.

GC: I'm interested in what you knew about art outside Italy. Alongside the system of galleries and museums, there is the circulation of books and art magazines. There weren't many of these in Italy at the time, however, and all information about what was going on internationally was carried in only a few publications.

LG: I remember contemporary art magazines like *Art International*, *Domus*, *Le Arti*, *Marcatre*, and *Collage*. American publications such as *Artforum*, *ARTnews*, and *Art in America* were available only by subscription. The galleries used to put out catalogues for every show, with an essay by a critic, and other catalogues were published by the Galleria d'Arte Moderna, which was directed by Palma Bucarelli.

GC: To continue with my interpretation of the dimension of movement, it seems clear to me that your work with variability, in framing devices and in the mobility demanded of the observer, is tied to cinema. Your first paintings progress from perception to action: to "read" the work involves moving sliding panels, almost like movie frames inserted one upon the other, to define a new image emerging from the "montage." Your panels thus establish a communication among variable wholes that refer to each other. They imply a slice of space and of image that changes its particular meaning when one panel is superimposed or flanked by another. The presence of the human figure is also a memory of movements of characters, almost like the fixed stage of the Chinese shadow theater, which, as we know, is a matrix for cinematography. But let's go back to the places and the artistic readings of the time.

LG: During that period we were also friends with many of the Italian film directors and with writers such as Italo Calvino, who had written the story for the film shot in Polynesia, *Tikoyo and the Shark*, which told the tale of a friendship between a shark and a Polynesian child. The film was produced by Titanus, which at the time was producing the most interesting films of Federico Fellini, Michelangelo

16

Antonioni, Francesco Maselli, Luchino Visconti, Francesco Rosi, Valerio Zurlini, and Gillo Pontecorvo. It was the era of the films of Antonioni and Monica Vitti, and of the books of Alain Robbe-Grillet; this was when *Last Year at Marienbad* was made, when François Truffaut, Jean-Luc Godard, Alain Resnais, and the other members of the *Nouvelle Vague* were working. These filmmakers often seemed to be addressing difficulties and problems in communication, and their mood influenced the way in which we were beginning to visualize reality in a different dimension, more detached and cool. At the Venice film festival, a journalist asked René Clair about the euphoria and general enthusiasm for the *Nouvelle Vague*, and he answered only, *"Chaque vague c'est une nouvelle vague."*

GC: Your attention to the *Nouvelle Vague* leads me to speak of visual perception, of the phenomenology that is the source of much '60s film. This was based on an antinaturalism of the glance, which turned itself over to the glass eye of the movie camera. What mattered was the registration of things and appearances, slowly canceling out the human presence. There was an attempt to avoid all psychological interpretation and every visceral dimension, to turn oneself over to a gnoseology of writing and of images. Every entity was seen through a lens that distanced and negated the romantic spirit of the work. Did your art reflect the presence of this *nouveau roman* attitude?

LG: For a while I was painting large canvases (not reproduced here) with a center similar to a camera lens: a circle or square containing an image. These works represent a character within the universe of appearances. They are like a world seen through a camera lens, a medium that emphasizes the reproduction of reality. Reality was revealed in the paintings, but was transformed by a hypothetical lens to become a symbol of representation. The central image in the lens was out of focus, more an impression than a real image. This was a world seen through a lens with an altered focal distance. The rest of the canvas, on the other hand, was filled with precise, meticulous diagrams and descriptions of all kinds of lenses, photographic calculations, times of exposure, aperture widths, and so on, all the media and methods that could eventually help to give focus to object and forms. These large canvases were divided into two or three parts, with the stretcher frames fixed to the wall, one next to the other. I did this to give the sense of sequences of images.

GC: Through the connection and concatenation of images, your "Variable Paintings" are also about time and the organic organization of painting. Personally,

I see them as a discourse on the relative dimensions of figures and representations, but also as a representation that carries with it the totality, the whole, and its parts. It's almost as if there were a quest for an active montage in which one could understand the immensity of the narrative implicit in a painting or other image. In this sense, the images mixed and filtered by a circular lens create a spiral of perspectives and accelerated communications, based on the dialectic of parts. What are the linguistic and philosophical principles, in addition to the mathematical ones, that govern these variable compositions?

LG: At the core of my "Variable Paintings" lies the desire to use the image over successive periods of time, to imbue the same image with different meanings. They are an attempt to move beyond the static structure of the canvas, making it mutable. Historically, the Futurist representation of the object in motion and the sequential images of Eadweard Muybridge's photographs can be seen as a common root for the "Variable Paintings." But I think of them as more related to the Bergsonian concept of "duration," to the idea of the interpretation of the image in a determined instant of time, which becomes the current instant, *the time of the work.* Also, I wanted to allow the spectator to participate in the work according to his or her own personal choice, to provide the opportunity to see the images of the painting in different "moments," with a variety of possible readings. Many levels of interpretation arise, depending on the movement created by spectators as they shift the sliding panels.

GC: You refer to Bergson and to his idea of movement as a passage from one moment to another, a sort of dance between object and spectator. The prehistory of cinema is also based on this mechanism of exchange and transfer between two entities, active and passive, which is why you point out Muybridge and Etienne Jules Maréy. Is art, then, an activity focused on a "moment" that is part of a larger sequence, or a series of the notable small "instants" of an artificial movement in which time is not represented but implied?

LG: In the "Variable Paintings" the work process was a dialogue that involved the viewer; it was a reaction to the accepted historical way of reading an artwork. I was looking for a way to have the work convey many different moments of perception, escaping the static condition of a univocal image. Culturally and conceptually, I was trying to reach another dimension, which the static surface of the canvas was unable to provide: a simultaneity of perceptions and images that achieved even greater shifts of meaning, depending on time and movement. Setting in motion figures and objects that represented a static moment, I wanted to erase the absence of time from my paintings, giving them a temporal dimension.

GC: Because of this open dimension of the work, your research tends to go beyond traditional linguistic frontiers, moving away from painting and arriving at installation and environmental art, with incursions into materials like Plexiglas and artificial fog. In the final analysis, you have moved toward the creation of a "field" of variable and indeterminate configurations. It is no accident that you tend to emphasize the movement internal to your work, both through the iteration of the same figure or sign and through the modification of the structure of the work to give it a kinetic dimension, a dissolution of its usual stasis. All this occurs a few years after the publication of Umberto Eco's *Opera Aperta*, in 1962, a book that deals with mobility, with ambiguity, and with the multiperspectival nature of meaning. What is your relationship with this theorizing, which informed an entire generation of poets like the Gruppo 63, and of artists like Pino Pascali?

LG: I only got to know those people in 1965, at a Gruppo 63 conference in Palermo. We were all together for a week, for meetings, meals, trips to the seaside, exhibitions, and concerts. (I remember music by Sylvano Bussotti and Kathy Berberian.) Inge Feltrinelli was there with the entire Gruppo 63, and I met Umberto Eco, Alberto Arbasino, Angelo Guglielmi, Furio Colombo, and the others. I had already read Arbasino's and Eco's books, Edoardo Sanguineti's poetry, and their writings in general. After that I saw them often in Rome (where many of them lived) at the house of Luisa Spagnoli, who was more or less at the center of things, a friend of artists and writers; or in Milan, at the houses of Ottiero Ottieri, Camilla Cederna, and the Feltrinellis, where I used to go with Beatrice Monti, who had shown my paintings at her gallery a few months earlier. Umberto Eco often came to our house and to my studio. I gave him a gouache that he called his portrait; it represented a pair of broken eyeglasses in a stylized geometric landscape (it was a sort of joke, to remind him how he had slipped in a puddle of water in Palermo, breaking his glasses, which he went about wearing that way during the days that followed). In response and in thanks, Umberto sent me a strange letter of four pages filled with adverbs, written in rows one below the other.

In Palermo, at the same conference, I got to know Pino Pascali. He sometimes came to visit me at home, where I had a large zebra skin on the floor, which I had brought back from Africa. One day he looked at it carefully, then made a gesture, tracing its outline in the air. Seeing that he was drawing it mentally, I gave him a pencil and a sheet of paper, but he once again slowly repeated the outline in the air, answering that he didn't need paper and pencil, the form was now imprinted in his mind and he would remember it. Some time later he made a piece, representing an animal skin with thick fur, that hung on the wall. I always wondered whether it was my zebra.

During that period I read *V* by Thomas Pynchon, *Le Degré zéro de l'écriture* by Roland Barthes (which impressed me deeply), and Herbert Marcuse. I also liked the theater pieces of Carmelo Bene; I particularly remember his *Pinocchio*.

GC: Working with the movement of bodies on a painted surface, you present the enigma between evidence and shadow, to the point where, in your work, the body remains silent and lets its reflection speak, a reflection that appears like an unknown, I would even say metaphysical force, which is also found in the superimposition of transparent surfaces and clouds. It is almost a moment of alienation from the physicality of the image, a quest for an unknown place that seems to come out of darkness, in the shadow, or out of light, in the clouds or the transparent surfaces. It is as if there were an artificial awakening where you seemed to have put things in order, establishing the walls, the furniture, the landscape where you project yourself, and where your existence now has an unnatural rather than a natural appearance. This attitude obviously implies a cold, "immaterial" feeling. These are objects suspended between dream and waking, in the movement of thought and of time.

LG: We can represent the same image in many different ways. It can be read on different levels depending on the surrounding circumstances. Each difference creates its own diversity of mental responses and perceptions. The shadow is used as an abstract representation of a human reality, and the hidden parts of the painting are used as different moments of the same reality, revealed and changed through the movement of the panels and through the presence and superimposition of the shadows.

GC: Your world—half internal self, half external reality—moves between a vision of your own being and the transparency of the context, and your technique is controlled and cool. It is as if you had renounced the corporeality of the hand to entrust yourself increasingly to a plan. This feeling is reinforced by the geometric and linear elements in your work, which are consistent with a controlled, programmed, almost "geometric" existence.

LG: The panels of my paintings were transparent openings to the outside world through a circle of lights and shadows shaping a geometric landscape. In this personal territory, I was playing a game of opposites: an image of myself was seen by the outside world, but at the same time the situation was reversed, and my image became the spectator. The painting was the stage for this dialectic, a cool description of a motionless figure that had an abstract presence, in a changeable configuration. The work had two levels of communication. It was a bidimensional world seen through a kaleidoscope, representing both the instant before movement and the instant after its transformation into another image.

GC: When and where did you show your first pieces, from 1964?

LG: I exhibited these works in 1965 at the Galleria dell'Ariete in Milan, with an essay by Renato Barilli in the accompanying catalogue, and then in group shows in Rome and at the Rome Quadriennale, where I was chosen for the young-artists section of the 1966 Venice Biennale. That same year I started the "Variable Paintings."

GC: At the previous Biennale, in 1964, the grand prize had gone to Robert Rauschenberg, and that year also marked the beginning of a widespread diffusion of American Pop art, with which many Italian artists sought a relationship. At first, this tendency led to the proposal of banal images, but later it was distinguished by a recourse to a more historical, less current iconography. Furthermore, if one thinks about the situation in Turin, with the presence of Michelangelo Pistoletto and Giulio Paolini, or of Luciano Fabro in Milan, one understands that Italian art of the time was engaging in a broad reflection on systems of making art and of confronting reality. Through terms of linguistic motivation and connection, it dealt with a transformation of the exterior situation at hand. What mattered was to keep oneself from being distracted by the outside appearance of everyday life and of mass consumption; instead, one had to stay with what lay behind this figure, and with its analysis and its deconstruction. This was the beginning of the philosophy of art that was to develop in the mid '60s. What is your relationship to the Pop generation in Rome and in Turin?

LG: The impressive exhibition of American Pop art at the 1964 Venice Biennale, curated by Alan Solomon, was the first I had seen of the work of those artists. I learned more about them when I went to New York two years later. Pistoletto, Enrico Castellani, Mario Ceroli, and I had been included in the Biennale in

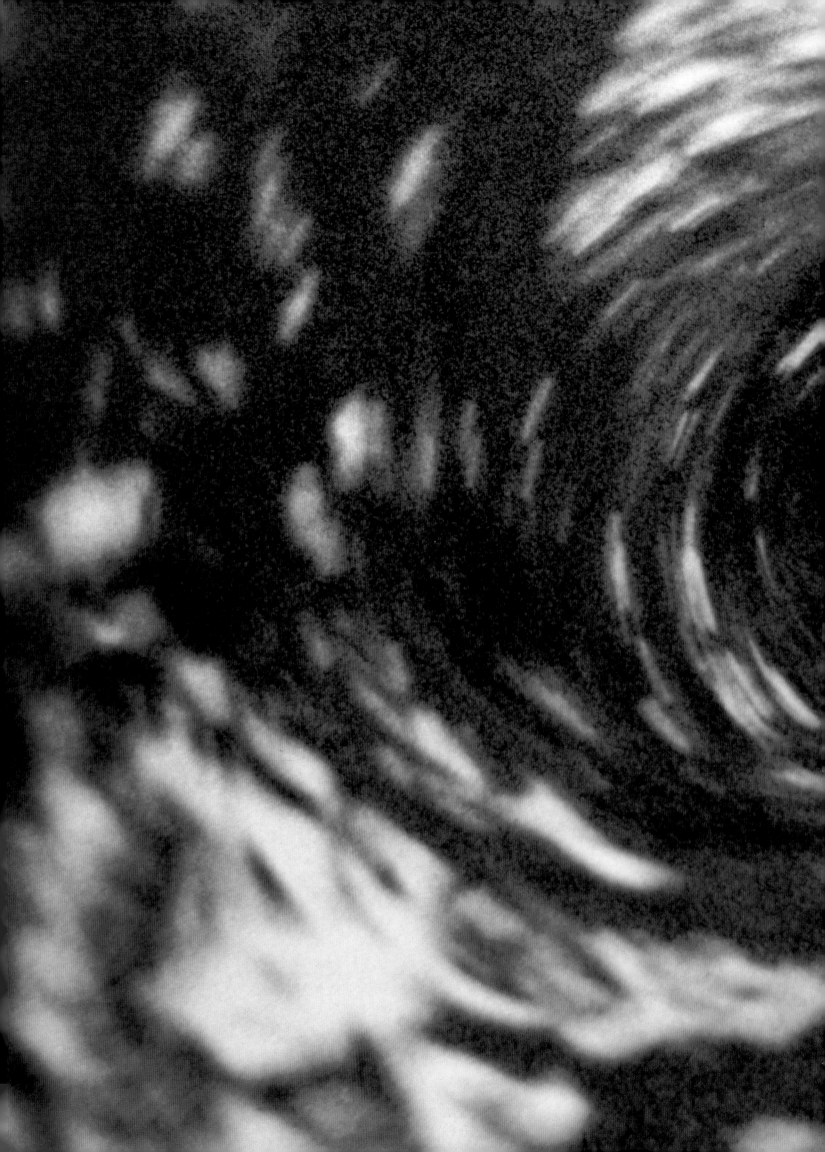

1966, where I showed my first "Variable Paintings."
There I met Leo Castelli—with his wife, Toini—and
Ileana Sonnabend for the first time; Leo liked the idea
that the sliding panels of my paintings were movable.
Through that exhibition I had my first group show in
New York, in October of that year. Organized by the
Bonino Gallery, the show was called "Italy New
Tendencies." I had never been to New York before.
Many important artists came to the opening—I
remember Barnett Newman there with Frank Stella
and Larry Poons, and also Alan Solomon, who then
decided to organize a larger American show of young
Italian artists. The following year he came to Italy
and chose the pieces for a group show at the Institute
of Contemporary Art in Boston—works by Kounellis,
Pistoletto, Valerio Adami, Getulio Alviani, Pascali,
Ceroli, and my "Neon Paintings." The show later
traveled to the Jewish Museum in New York, and
there I met Leo Castelli again, looking at my neon
works. The next time I met him was in Boston, in
1971, at the "Earth Air Fire Water" exhibition at the
Museum of Fine Arts, in which I showed my water
pieces. Two years later Leo Castelli gave me my first
exhibition at his gallery.

During my 1966 visit I went to see Roy Lichtenstein,
who showed me some of the work in his studio. And I
visited Jim Rosenquist, who was painting a huge
piece, and went to Andy Warhol's Factory, which was
crowded with his friends. I remember that the walls
were entirely covered in a brilliant silver material.
I also saw an extraordinary series of events at the
Armory Show, in which Rauschenberg and other
artists were performing, each for an evening, and
to see these performances was a really amazing
experience.

In Rome, the Tartaruga gallery, which was located
above Rosati's in the Piazza del Popolo, showed the
work of young Italian artists. Plinio De Martiis and
his wife, Nini Pirandello, owned the gallery, and it
was the center around which the Roman intellectual
world turned during that period. Every evening
artists and writers met there, including Alberto
Moravia, Goffredo Parise, Arbasino, Schifano,
Kounellis, Ceroli, and Pascali. I remember that I saw
there Tano Festa's *Persiane* (Wooden Shutters),
Franco Angeli's *Quarto di dollaro* (Quarter Piece),
and Schifano's *Il Futurismo rivisitato* (Futurism
Revisited). Soon after this Pascali left the gallery to
show his "cannons" at Gian Enzo Sperone's space in
Turin. *Arte povera* was born, with artists from Turin,
Milan, and Rome—and the center shifted.

Plinio closed his gallery during the summer of 1968,
after a final series of shows entitled *"Teatro delle
mostre"* (Theater of Exhibitions), where I showed

Wind Room. It was a time of worldwide student protests—a period of illusion, as it turned out—and there was an atmosphere of confrontation everywhere. Roman students loved the poet Giuseppe Ungaretti; a newspaper named four of them "the birds," because every day they climbed a tree facing his house and roosted there until evening, rhythmically chanting "Giuseppe! Giuseppe!" When Plinio closed the gallery he opened a bar behind the Piazza del Popolo, and the same crowd that had frequented his gallery went there every evening. Ungaretti also dropped in occasionally, and he came to my studio, with Piero Dorazio, to see my "*Antinebbia*" (Antifog) pieces, which he called "*colonne luminose a pareti*" (luminous walled columns). He came back to see them surrounded by artificial fog in the installation in the Marlborough gallery.

GC: From 1966 on you began to incorporate fluorescent tubing in your work, evoking a practice of the advertising culture and of commercial display. I am sure that you were aware of Chryssa's and Dan Flavin's use of the same material beginning in 1963–64, the former manipulating it as writing, the latter as a tautological entity. Both were interested in this technological and informational totem. Chryssa used it to construct a sequence of paginations, while Flavin was more struck by the possibility of aniconic, primary combinations. Around 1966, other artists like Mario Merz and Bruce Nauman also began to make use of neon. Were you aware of these developments, and how did you perceive them?

LG: Flavin's use of industrially produced fluorescent tubing is part of a discourse that pertains to Minimalism. Chryssa's neon is more monumental, a large technological sign. Nauman drew with neon, writing out his own name, for example. I remember seeing his work for the first time, in New York in 1968. Merz also wrote an ideological phrase on an igloo piece, which I saw in a show in Rome that same year; then, with his series of Fibonacci numbers, he too was writing and drawing with these luminous signs.

When I began to use neon, in 1966, I wanted a material that was technologically defined but that I could still use in a craftsmanlike way. With neon, I wanted to obtain different gradations of the same color, distributing the gas and curving the tube in which it was sealed according to the result that I wanted to achieve. I wanted to create effects of depth, to exploit light for its possibilities of refraction, to create dimension and an artificial perspective, a three-dimensional painting in neon.

GC: It seems to me that your explorations led you toward a certain "pictorialism," that is, you worked with the visual metamorphosis of colors and of the environment that fluorescent tubing creates. It is, again, a discourse on the passage between day and night, where the city, with its shop windows and its signs, continues to dominate.

LG: My neon paintings reflect the impact of the nighttime environment of the city, the constellations of hundreds of luminous signs, the striped and colored Plexiglas, the advertising, the fluorescent light, the steel and aluminum, the illuminated windows with backlit shadows through the glass. The figures in the works are closed off in that world of neon signs and lights. Representing the psychological oppression of the urban environment, they see landscape as an artificial universe, in which reality is only an illusionary duplicate. The works define the boundary of that open arena. The life-sized figures appear and disappear, opaque and mysterious, subjects and objects seen through transparencies and lights, framed in a three-dimensional space of simultaneous flatness and depth.

GC: In *Racing Car Room*, 1967, you use the silhouettes of racing cars, as you had used your own and others' silhouettes and shadows in previous works. It is as if the theme of the velocity of communication, or of the passage of shadows, were connected to the speed of the automobile. This is clearly a continuation of your recourse—almost a Futurist recourse—to Italian art history, seen, however, in the perspective of contemporary culture.

LG: The challenge of the laws of mechanics, dynamics, and gravity was what interested me—the power, the speed, the design of formula-one cars. To imprison an image of movement in a transparent box, to block it and transform it into a static object. I wanted to see a lot of these cars together in one room, a silent competition of immobile racing cars in a delimited space, closed off by the wall.

GC: From 1968 on, a certain artificial "naturalism" works its way into your art. I am thinking of your "*Antinebbia*" series, the "antifog" columns of neon conceived to be installed in a natural context such as a meadow. They are extraneous to the context, yet they add an element to nature, are a further replication of it, although they are urban in tone. If I look carefully at them, these tall towers surrounded by fog end up seeming like skyscrapers on a reduced scale. But they are also the departure point for your experiments with natural elements, where contrasts and elisions between parts are used to discover a dualistic view between the extremes of the natural and the unnatural.

LG: I wanted to produce natural elements

artificially, provoking a psychological metamorphosis that would redefine a space. This was due in part to my experiences in nature during my travels, almost a rediscovery for me of natural phenomena, with monsoons in Asia, rain on the atolls, refraction in the desert. I did several works using fog, wind, air, and rain, and I called them the "Natural Elements" series.

I had just finished the "Neon Paintings" series, in which I transmitted signs of the urban environment, figures imprisoned as if in glass booths, malaise, incommunicability, the ambiguity between the backlit figure and the spectator. Then I wanted to use natural elements, liberated from structure, to bring the same spectator into a more human, more free condition, to give him or her the possibility, within a cultural context, to hear once again the sound of the rain, isolated, presented as a new experience, or to feel the wind, or to see that the air is a presence, that there are stars and rainbows as well as the noise of the city and the lights of advertising. This is why I "artificially" recreated phenomena as naturally as possible, not contained inside a painting or three-dimensional object. I wanted to involve the visitor and to experiment with the elements in a physical way, letting the spectator participate in the physical quality of the element itself, which was made provocative by its reproduction in a context as different from the space of nature as the space of a gallery. I didn't want a painting or a sculpture containing air, earth, or water; I didn't want air, earth, or water to become objects; I wanted to recreate the experience of natural phenomena.

GC: In 1967, the Attico Gallery in Rome held a show entitled "*Fuoco Immagine Terra Acqua*" (Fire Image Earth Water), in which Kounellis and Pascali exalted primordial elements like earth, fire, and water. Did you see the show, and what was your position in respect to its naturalistic representations, its puddles and its daisy of fire?

LG: I remember that show. I was primarily interested in the less material, less tangible quality of the elements—using them to create feelings and moods rather than objects. I was using fog, wind, air, rainbows, stars, refractions, whirlpools, and rain.

GC: What is surprising and unusual is your use of fog or wind in an enclosed space, as if you wanted to charge the traditional territory of art, the gallery and the museum, with the immaterial effects of a natural phenomenon.

LG: They are interventions to modify the structure of a space with the presence of a natural element. The "fog" becomes form, participating in the definition of

the space, modifying it with its presence. The "wind" is unexpected in a closed space, as is the "rain" that drips from a pipe in a room, and the sound of its drops, and the volume of water into which it falls, stirring the surface with circles of ripples. And to experience the dizzying depth and concentric velocity of a whirlpool in a closed environment alters that environment's prerogative. Likewise air, colorless and transparent, isn't usually noticed as a presence, though it is omnipresent, so I wanted to define it visually through a perimeter of light.

GC: A visual vertigo comes out of putting fog and fluorescent tubing together; there is a perceptual similarity between the two, both operating on a principle of "fine dust," of particles that reflect or radiate light. What lies behind this interweaving of the immaterial and the imperceptible? Does your use of these effects in an interior space also imply an alteration of the architectural container? What is the analogy between the concrete, realized objects and their existence as images?

LG: In the "*Antinebbia*" pieces, my last neon pieces, which I did in January 1968, I added artificial fog to create a further effect of refraction, through which the light filtered—broken, refracted, visible and invisible at the same time. The neon was in different gradations of color, from a blue violet to a near white that was absorbed by the white of the fog. I was working at reproducing natural elements in an enclosed space, to alter the space's structure with something extraneous to it. The fog was the first of these outdoor elements that I transferred indoors.

GC: Together with the experience of the nontactile, you present an experience of the world as an infinite production of images, as aggregates of fragile, changeable states—a forest or a landscape where the human being is "reflected." In 1968, the same year that you began your investigations into the passages of nature, you embarked on another series of travels, which triggered profound reactions in your work. It seems to me that the most important of these was your journey to Africa. How did this come about, and why? What were the consequences of your exposure to Africa's almost invincible, intangible sort of nature, as opposed to the relatively domesticated European landscape?

LG: We went to Africa to find locations for part of a film that Folco was shooting on the continent's history. We visited Nigeria, the Sahara, Niger, Upper Volta, Dahomey, and then we went to Chad.

There was a piece that I wanted to do at the time, recreating the effect of refraction in water, but I didn't know where or how to do it. I imagined it in a large expanse of water, which couldn't, however, be very deep. Then I arrived at Lake Chad. With the sunlight reflecting on the water, the lake seemed like an infinite flat surface. Dazzling, immobile, it stretched as far as the horizon. I didn't know it yet, but Lake Chad, one of the largest lakes in the world, is also the shallowest of any approaching its size. I had found the place I was looking for to make my *Refraction* piece.

One afternoon in the Sahara, about two hours before sunset, the sun's rays were shining in a kind of diagonal light, and we saw a mirage. On the horizon, the sand dunes appeared to be reflected in a water surface on which a man and two camels were slowly walking. The sand dunes were reflected upside down, reversed. I took a picture of the mirage, and was surprised later when I saw it exactly reproduced in my color photograph; in a way, I had expected that this immaterial, nonexistent image could not be recorded on film.

A few hours later we arrived at an oasis, with nomads and camels, and I understood that this was where the images I had seen before had come from. The oblique rays of the sun had created the effect of a mirrored surface on the sand, producing a refraction effect, and the image had appeared some miles away from where the real scene actually was.

Doing the work on Lake Chad, using the effects of the sunlight's refraction on the water, I remembered its refraction on the sand dunes. They were both optical illusions, and I wanted to recreate them both in an indoor space.

GC: The use of the properties of desert and water implies an attempt to reappropriate the mobility of the material. Placed indoors, they create a "false" reality. If I connect them to the "Variable Paintings," I notice that the shadow and the reality seem to change roles: there, the shadow haunts reality, almost as something external to it, and here the shadow moves in "spirit" and matter, light and water. But the spectator remains the subject, remains at the center of the interpretation. In the "Variable Paintings," the spectator is inside the action; in the environment, he or she is literally surrounded by the artistic event. The spectacle is no longer sustained through sliding, alterable "sets," but through the force and the energy of natural effects.

In *Rain Room*, 1968, we again find ourselves faced with an operation on the "void," a further metaphysical turn in which there is an emphasis on nature's will to exist.

Following pages: photographs from the artist's travels. Left to right, top to bottom: Children's initiation ceremony, village of Boni, Upper Volta; the bobò masks represent forest gods and wild animals. Peul shepherds prove their courage in the sha-ròt ceremony, Niger. Men of the Tuareg, the blue-veiled nomads of the Sahara. The king of Abomey, Dahomey. The pyramid of Cheops. The astronomical observatory of Raja Djay Singh, from the mid-18th century, Delhi. The sundial in the Delhi observatory. Ennedi plateau, Chad. A nomad and "his mosque" (a stone square in the desert), Saudi Arabia. Mudmen in ritual mud masks, New Guinea. Muslim warrior dance, Sulu Islands. And vintas, the distinctive boats of the Badjaos, the nomads of the sea, Mindanao.

LG: I wanted to create the natural effect of the sound of water falling in water, to create an environment where one might meditate, listening to the noise of the rain. Above, there was a pipe from which water dripped constantly; below, there was a large shallow basin. The level of the water in the basin was flush with the floor of the rest of the environment, like a small lake in a room where one could sit and hear only the sound of a natural element, closed off from the rest of the world. When I remade *Rain Room* with my piece *Drops of Water* in the Boston Museum of Fine Arts, in 1971, I saw young people seated on the floor around the basin in a circle, listening to the falling drops and looking at the ripples that ruffled the water's surface in a continuous, always changing pattern.

My travels in Africa were also an opportunity to work on a wind piece for which I explored a selection of air currents—different types of wind, at different velocities, in different situations. During a storm in the Sahara, the blowing of the wind and the swirling of the sand had created such a compact material effect that it made me consider wind in a completely objective way. I decided to compare this element in a variety of environments, many different winds blowing at many different speeds. I started documenting their effects through a camera, and also recorded their sounds. I collected a number of images of different winds in several countries and in a variety of types of location—in the ocean, in fields, in the trees of the forest, in the city. That same year, 1968, I decided to reproduce a particular wind speed—40 knots—with a wind machine in the closed environment of a gallery, altering the usual connotations of its space. In *Wind Room*, I again brought the feeling of an element of outside space into an architectural interior.

GC: In *Air Room*, 1968, one is made conscious that the "void" of our everyday atmosphere is the vehicle of a luminosity and a sensory quality that pass through it constantly. Here there is a quest for the minimal, imperceptible presence of the vibrations of the air. It is almost an experience without stimuli, where one is pushed to listen to oneself, to be aware of oneself. Reducing image references as much as possible, and polarizing one's sensory and analytic awareness of simple facts of structure and context, sound and light, you seem to push the body from the perception of external objects to that of internal processes, so that one's responses exalt one's inner senses and their modes of association.

LG: *Air Room* is the spatial and volumetric reflection of a thin thread of light that gives an imaginary, almost visually perceived consistency to a

30

volume of air. It is an osmosis between a technological medium such as neon light and a natural element such as air, whose specific characteristics are colorlessness, transparency, and immateriality. Yet air can acquire a volumetric visual texture by being focused through artificial light, which defines its form and solidifies its shape.

GC: At times, you create a dialectic between day and night, light and dark, body and shadow, through the use of other symbolic materials, for example the lead and light of *Star Room*, 1968. Since ancient times, lead has been the material that emerges from and represents darkness, blackness, night. In addition, its malleability symbolizes a motility of materials. In this piece the lead is melted by the heat of the light, which slowly moves beyond its two-dimensional boundary and makes the space fecund, giving birth to a system of "stars."

LG: At first I wasn't sure whether to use a wall of lead or of tin to create my wall of stars in *Star Room*. I decided I liked lead better. It's more interesting, because it's a contradictory material: soft and extremely malleable, which usually suggests lightness, but dark and heavy.

Behind the wall of lead there were special tiny high-intensity light bulbs, partly laminated in gold on the inside. These lamps melted small holes at different points in the lead, a few at a time, over the entire wall, letting rays of light filter into the rest of the space. These beams took the form of stars, because of the diffraction effect. In the end, the entire room was full of stars.

GC: In *Rainbow*, 1968, another strong image enters your work. It is a sign of the mediation between high and low, between one world and another. It also represents an example of transference from one attribute to another, a path between two entities. As in the other rooms, the path or passage that you intend or that you seem to want to communicate is the transformation of technological mechanisms into natural ones. You create first the stars, then the rainbow, both with artificial light. In the final analysis, the aspiration is for the union of opposites, of the natural and the artificial. I see the same impulse in your alliance between fog and neon. This was a pressing subject in the early '60s, when the traditional humanist culture of the West realized that it was being inundated with the effects of the mass media. It attempted a renewal and an integration, with art trying to function as the bridge.

LG: My purpose in *Rainbow* was to create a horizon at eye level, traversing the four walls of a room, and

making visible all the colors of the spectrum that the air, which is colorless, lets pass through. I obtained this effect by shining a light through a prism, which is the simplest, most elementary way to decompose the colors of the spectrum. What I wanted was to have a rainbow inside a room.

GC: The transit or the transition between one element and another is also represented in your use of photography, which mediates between the photographer and what is photographed, establishing more relationships between natural states and artificial ones—the photographing subject and its camera, the photographed subject and what appears in the frame. Once again we have a dual situation, an attempt at osmosis. In the book *Distillations: Choice and Choosing 16 from 5000* there is also a passage from a naturalistic aspect to an anthropological one. The images are those you gathered during your journeys between 1960 and 1973. They are another way in which you captured the movement of your travels, and a recourse to another artificial language, that of representation, of simulation. In addition, I see another dialectic established within the visual result. To present the photographs and their subjects, you create a very precise grid that visually "structures" this explosion of images, which are rich in magnificent visual elements and information. Is this another intermediary moment?

LG: Distillation as procedure: an extract of visual, mental, spiritual experiences. These photographs were the result of the impact on me of many different cultures, with their various rituals and modes of behavior in various cultural contexts and traditions. They were also the sum of my personal reactions to a wide range of environmental situations. I was interested in finding affinities between ethnic groups that were both very different from each other and also often alike, with similar mythologies, rituals, customs, and habits, although occurring in countries quite distant from each other. In the cordillera of the Andes, for example, I saw the last surviving symbols of the Inca culture mixed with symbols introduced by the infiltration of Catholic missionaries: the *hombre pajaro*, the birdman, is an Indian who represents a bird symbol and is covered with colored feathers, but he carries a cross, and leads the Easter procession to Tilcara, 13,000 feet up in the Andes. Likewise, animist rituals along the Atlantic coast of Dahomey include symbols found on the other shore of the Atlantic, in the *macumba* rite of Brazil. The initiation rites and the masks occur in different cultures, but have the same matrix. Then there's the covered face: from the blue *litham* veil of the Tuareg chiefs to the mud masks that cover the faces of the mudmen in New Guinea, or to the silver mask that covers only

Distillations: Choice and
Choosing 16 from 5000 *(details),*
1970: "Flight"

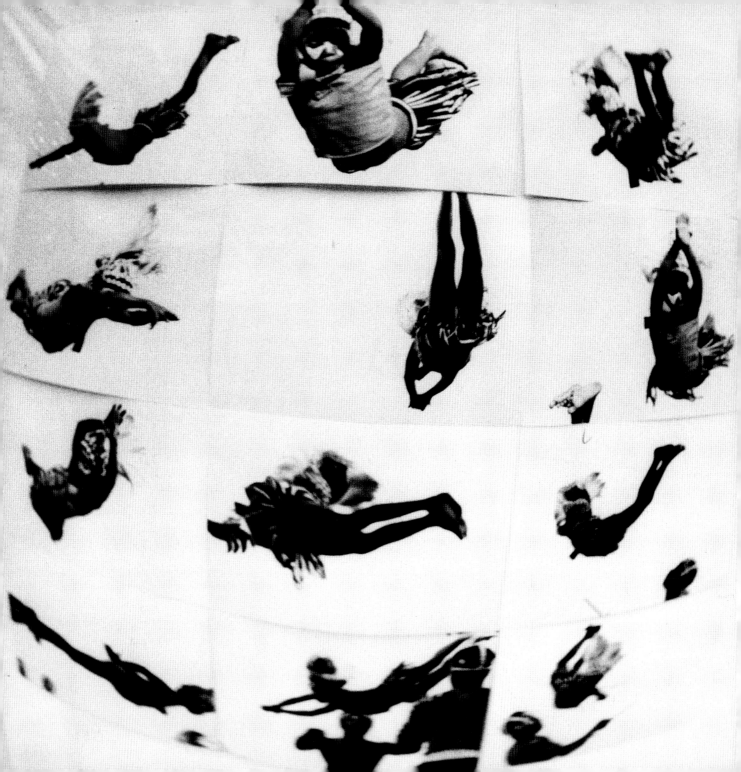

the nose of the king of Abomey. This latter example has a mystical purpose, since the king's subjects believe they are hearing from his mouth the voices of their ancestors, venerated as divinities. I also found a system of oral traditions present in both Asiatic and Polynesian culture, with the shaman and the *warepo*, both having the task of keeping alive the memory of their history and mythology, from the Tiki to the oceanic transmigrations.

Distillation as a selection among a large number of images, provoking personal reactions and meditations. The present of the present, the present of the past, the present of the future, which is discussed by Saint Augustine. Distillation as a meditative quality: the counting of grains of sand as a measurement of time, sand and spiral a suggestion of infinity, the spiral as unending circular motion, representing endless time. This work, *The Measuring of Time*, 1969, was the first of my three "Distillations" pieces, inspired by travels through several deserts. The second, *Distillations: 3 Months of Looking*, 1970, was a piece I made during travels in places like the Leeward Islands, Malaysia, the Philippines, the Sulu Islands, and the New Hebrides; it was an analysis of my personal, visual, and physical sensations. The third piece, *Distillations: Choice and Choosing 16 from 5000*, 1970, was a collection and selection of images from earlier trips, like a grid of different realities restructured in a single image.

GC: The reconciliation between different and opposite interlocutors is a recurring notion in the history of Western metaphysics; the condition of something midway between beautiful and ugly, nocturnal and diurnal, is the attempt to fill the gap. *Choice and Choosing 16 from 5000* takes what were first photographic "remains," a body of around 5,000 images, and makes them into a book. It is almost as though you wanted to communicate to the reader another, different approach to your experience. As in the "Variable Paintings," the idea is to circulate the image, leaving the spectator free to travel within it. Is this another passage?

LG: It was almost a necessary linguistic choice. I really wanted an object to leaf through, one image after another, to be perceived in successive moments, in the dimension of the page. *Distillations: 3 Months of Looking* was about sensations and experiences I had had on different physical and psychological levels that I wanted to describe, making them available to be repeated by those who might find themselves in similar conditions of place, time, and environmental circumstance. It was almost an analysis that could be repeated as an experiment. The same criterion holds for *Choice and Choosing 16 from 5000*. Photography was necessary here in two ways: first, as a technical means for gathering images and materials during numerous voyages; secondly, to create the assemblage of images, to restructure them successively in a single photo, providing a unity of place and of time that is, precisely, the purpose of the work.

GC: The selection is made among 5,000 images; how did the associations and juxtapositions come about? What visual analogies did you want to establish in the structure of the individual groups?

LG: The 16 groups of photos that are the subject of the work are selected from around 5,000 photographs taken during several years of travel. I chose them by several different criteria, including size, location, subject matter, time of year, number of objects, similarities in shape, affinities in content, and so on. For each of the 16 groups I used a different method of choosing, introducing a variety that forces the viewer to read the photos comparatively rather than out of the more habitual kind of visual response. Because I made my selection on the basis of a variety of formal and other affinities, each of the 16 groups became an assemblage apparently having the same linguistic value. In reality, however, the differences between and within them are enormous, because the photographs belong to different countries and different cultures, and were taken with different cameras and lenses at different times in different years. So I decided to create a unique image-symbol that could unify each group, by rephotographing it with a single lens, at a single time, in a single place. As Claude Lévi-Strauss said, "I believe that content never has a meaning in itself—it is only the way in which the different elements are combined together which gives them a meaning."

GC: You're interested in dance, which is also a way of organizing an explosive subject, the body, in sequences and in combinations of almost mathematical order. Dance is a classical manifestation of movement. It represents rhythm and establishes a harmony of gestures, regulating the organic magma, causing one image to slide into another.

LG: Classical dance is a sequence of calculated movements regulated by very precise, perhaps mathematical harmonious laws. Clearly, gravity and equilibrium are among the elements of dance, among the components to be analyzed; for me, they constitute its essential value. This is true for both classical and modern dance, although in the latter realm I have seen completely antigravitational performances. And then music is also tied to mathematics, especially contemporary music. I remember a page that Philip Glass gave me from the score of his *Changing Parts*. It was a true page of mathematics, with precise repetitions and variations of the same alphabetical letter, numbered and repeated according to his scheme.

GC: In *Equilibrium: To Carlotta Grisi*, 1971, why were you interested in reducing the movements of the body to lines and arcs?

LG: Because I wanted a synthesis of the movements of dance, their image no longer organic but abstract.

GC: Why did you choose an image from a ballet of 1843?

LG: I chose this image because it represented a new movement in dance, the *pas de quatre* of Carlotta Grisi. One of the most interesting steps in the history of classical ballet, the *pas de quatre* coordinates four dancers in a single movement; it is almost an abstract concept. Théophile Gautier was so taken with Grisi's *pas de quatre* that he wrote a poem for her.

GC: The traces of dance movements led you to define a series of right angles and diagonals—why?

LG: This is my interpretation of dance. I wanted to imagine successive movements as diagonal lines. In my drawings for *Equilibrium*, the lines that form acute angles, right angles, arches, and semicircles, and the spheres suspended from these lines, are all imagined as in motion. Then they stop, in positions that challenge gravity; and then they return to their movement. It is a calculated alternation of motion and stasis, according to a measured rhythm, like dance steps.

GC: After the presentation of definite outlines in your early work, you moved on to elements characterized by indeterminacy and indistinctness, like sound and the ocean. These are entities without form, again a condition between extremes, like transparency and darkness.

LG: Living for some months on a Polynesian atoll, Rangiroa, during the rainy season, I developed a new sensitivity to the rain, to the rhythmic sound of drops falling constantly on the flat surface of the lagoon, in the center of the atoll, mixed with the sound of the Pacific waves breaking on the reef. My work *Drops and Ocean* derived from that experience. Later, I decided to incorporate that work in the piece *Sounds*, 1971, which attempted to capture the effects of sound by presenting them in the form of a commercial product: an object like a cassette tape, to be used as artwork/entertainment.

GC: You move from the diffuse, unplaceable sound of the water and the ocean to the positioning of stones. This is a passage toward another dialectical condition. The stones' fall, one after another, symbolizes sedimentation and construction. Thus it is no wonder that you combine them, setting up interrelationships among them, almost as if they formed a cyclical crystallization. Furthermore, stone is a passive material upon which to impose human activity, yet another reason for manipulating them and for organizing them according to intellectual and numerical variations. In ancient times the stone was a symbol of consciousness, a dynamic instrument of conceptual activity, always in terms of the interweaving between the artificial, what is built with the mind, and the natural.

LG: After *Sounds* I actually did a series of works, "Variations in Space," some of which were based on pebbles. I devised a mental and visual system for arranging a small number of pebbles in a great number of different combinations. I also used coins and other objects. The pebbles were used as part of a codification that gave a different linguistic value to a natural material. The stone became an abstract object, a numerical entity. Arranging five pebbles in every mathematical permutation of their sequence, there is the possibility of 120 different combinations in the same space. The piece is a reflection on the data of reality applied to a finite number of stones, to give a different order to natural objects. It reminds me of Galileo's description of nature: "Nature is like a book of infinite pages; the language in which it is written is mathematics, and its letters are geometrical figures."

GC: Photographic sequence, cinema, and dance all deal with "nonfixed" values, movements, distributed in space and in time. It is, then, a self-evident step for you to move into film and video work. This evolution bears witness to the reciprocal action between parts, your hand and its organic movement affecting the "static" movement of the stones.

LG: I made the video/film piece about a year earlier, in 1972. It was a way for me to have direct contact with action in nature: working actually in a stone quarry, I chose four stones from the multitude, then used them as an arithmetic symbol, methodically giving them an order, a different code from the one they had had before.

GC: From the rainbow to the sequenced bands of color in *Stripes*, 1974, from the natural element (although artificially recreated) to the drawing of individual colored stripes, almost like the creation of an infinite chromatic score, a two-dimensional rainbow. The colors also represent the elements and space, and

therefore a further transportation from one territory to another. It is as if the metamorphosis and the encounter between two truths or two souls of our culture were meant to bring about this new "subject." In the process from one to the other, through abstract formalizations or through concrete realizations, your work aspires to point out a reciprocal tension, a creation of images of thought, which are the "new" reality.

LG: With *Stripes* I returned to the rainbow, this time not as a natural phenomenon but as an analysis of color and of all the possible different juxtapositions that six colors can have, alternating in the same space: a scroll of Japanese canvas. Why this scroll? Because the work has a meditative quality that I associate with the spirit of Zen. The abstract indifference of the work's method also reminds me of Zen. I arranged stripes of the three primary and three complementary colors in their 720 different possible combinations, examining and drawing them all. I ascertained that there were these many possibilities, no more, no less.

GC: This phase of your work is tied to the slipping by of the moments, to the constellation, and the imperceptible nature, of time. One piece, *Hypothesis about Time*, 1975, makes the theme explicitly visual in the watch face, which is photographed so as to document segments of time, a temporal sequence of time. You make visible the mental and visual experience of the passing moments, giving physicality to an immaterial condition.

LG: As physical objects, the clocks serve the purpose, in their stasis (because fixed in a photographic image), of visualizing a different measure of time. Each of them records a different second, motionless, as a negation of the movement of time—they are the fantasy, the duplicate, of the real unit of temporal measure. Together they embody a hypothesis of time in which the past, the present, and the future switch their usual serial order into a new cycle of repetition: the future anticipates the past, altering time's supposedly unidirectional flow. As Marshall McLuhan says, "The future is a thing of the past." The enigmatic nature of time has fascinated artists and thinkers from ancient Greece to Bergson, with his theory of duration: "The only real dimension of time is its duration as an instantaneous fact of knowledge." Borges too wrote, "Time doesn't exist except as time perceived by someone."

GC: And how does the interaction between past and present, before and after, manifest itself in this work?

LG: I applied a mathematical system of permutation

to groups of three different seconds, obtaining a variation of the unidirectional serial order in which time goes. The images of the seconds of the clock move backward as well as forward, in a passage of time in which future and past switch order and direction.

GC: Time and its linearity are not iconic, so that they can be put down in "abstract" images or figures—geometrical figures such as the hexagon or the triangle.

LG: The hexagon is a geometric figure with multiple equivalencies. I have always imagined labyrinths as hexagons placed one next to the other, forming figures in which every intersection is like a corridor impossible to exit. To multiply the lines of a hexagon by the addition of other hexagons is to multiply it each time by six squared. The shape is the geometric figure that is closest to the *aleph*, the number to which one can add or subtract any number and its value doesn't change.

I used the hexagon in my *Hypothesis about Space*, 1975, a continuous rotation of the form from one to infinity, always identically repeated, in a perspective in which the continuity of space and the movement in time provide the possibility of infinite repetition. For me, the hexagon rotation also has a symbolic relationship with the continuity of the melodic structure of the rondo, which is an unending, circular melodic rhythm, repeating itself continuously.

I also used hexagons in *Scheherazade*, 1972, which is a materialization of the dream of Chuang Tzu, from an ancient Chinese text. One night he dreamed he was a yellow butterfly, and as a butterfly he could see himself as Chuang Tzu, sleeping. Yet at the same time, Chuang Tzu was flying about as the butterfly. It was a mirrored dream in which he was his own double. And my butterfly in *Scheherazade* is closed in a hexagonal space that is repeated, doubled, and multiplied, and that the prismatic vision of the butterfly makes even more labyrinthine and infinite.

GC: Your works always seem directed toward a "control" of the possible permutations of mental or physical data, almost like an infinite outline of moves that, however, must remain open. Examined in the inverse, this suggests an inner control of the self, a theater of "interior" organization in which one must accept the alternation of parts. In *Endless Dialogue*, 1977, you make use of the chessboard, the richest, most open symbol of this mobile duality: it has the white and the black (like day and night), velocity and control, linear and diagonal progress, but it always remains a coherent, controlled system. The chessboard

Following pages:
Endless Dialogue *(detail), 1977*

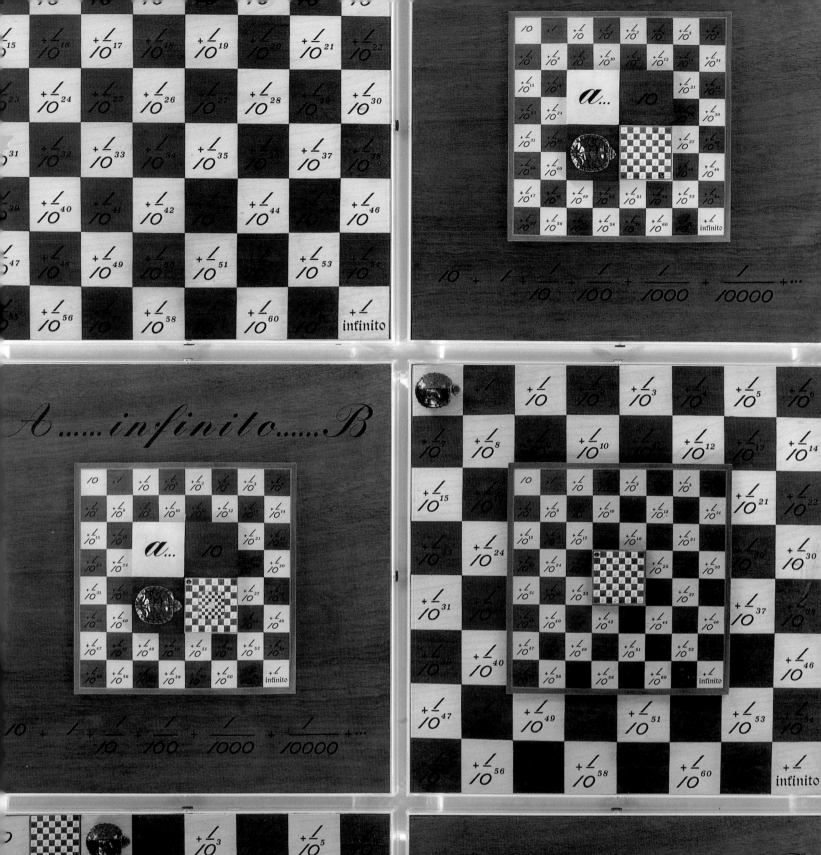

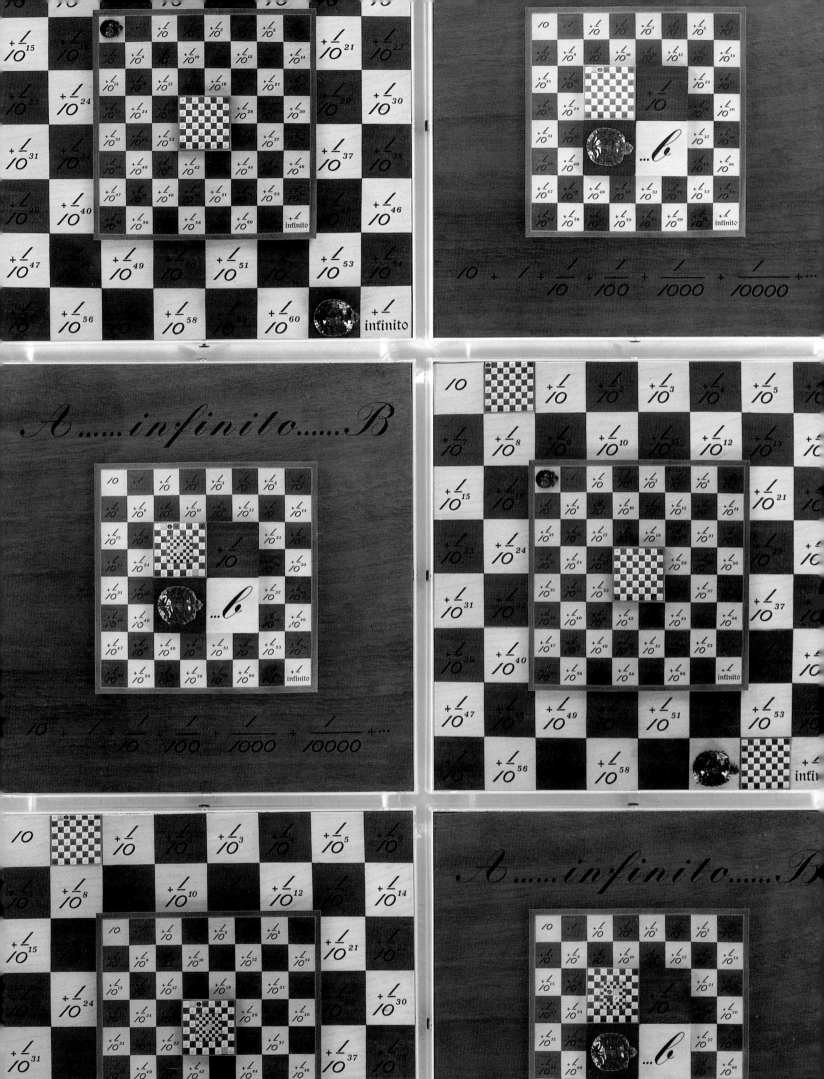

fascinated Marcel Duchamp because it is an instrument of infinite significances, all of which can be found in a single element. I also think here of the permutations of the I Ching, which has been used in contemporary art by John Cage, among others.

LG: I think of *"De More Geometrico"* (the group of my works that includes *Endless Dialogue*) as a world of geometric forms in a continuity of space that is always divisible into smaller spaces. The movement becomes a progression through distances that withdraw into infinitely divisible extensions. As Zeno said, "If everything that exists is in space, space itself must be in space, and so on ad infinitum."

I used the surface of a chessboard as a territory in which to extend my working process. The chessboard as an image has always interested me for its linguistic significance, which is related to its great number of possibilities of arrangement and movement. I used it as an object, in actual size, with a small green tortoise. My chessboard is a surface divisible into forever smaller spaces; it is crossed by a tortoise, which, before reaching the last square, faces another infinitely divisible square: another chessboard. The last border will never be reached. It is an idea of a route that has a clear beginning but no end.

I don't play chess, but I am fascinated by the process of the game, with all its possibilities and its permutability of movement. It is a structure in which two people confront each other philosophically and intellectually. I know that Cage played chess with Duchamp. I cannot imagine a greater confrontation, Duchamp's world and Cage's world facing each other. Both have extended the boundary of what can be understood as art. And Cage introduced the idea of using random occurrences and random sounds as the basis for artistic and musical composition.

GC: Organizing a show and exhibiting your work means bringing about a structural transformation of time and space, of both individual and cultural experience. In other words, it implies a setting in motion of relationships that are internal and external to your pieces, which are in themselves relationships and transmissions. What does it mean to you to set up an exhibition, to utilize a space or a sequence of works, to place a progression of figures or groupings within an architectural space?

LG: Each work needs its own psychological space, on which its physical space depends. I am talking about environmental installations. I always thought that my hexagon works should be installed in a hexagonal space, as they finally were. An installation can be created depending on the way a work needs to be perceived. Some works can be read in different ways: my chessboard piece has been installed in a line around the entire length of the walls of a space, but it could also be installed as a big square composed of all the square chessboards, becoming an enormous chessboard itself. A work can fill the space entirely, can become part of the space, or can even give an illusionistic quality to the space itself.

I have planned three installations that dealt with space in this latter sense. The first, from 1971, the most physical of the three, would consist of a perfectly level floor divided into two halves, one covered in wood painted with a bright enamel, the other covered in water dyed the same color. A perfect plane, an identical color. Under the lights, the two different materials would look the same, giving the illusion of a unique surface entirely filling the space.

I'm also interested in perspectives that give space a different viewpoint from that of classical perspective. The second installation, from 1977, was related to this idea. It was designed as a space to be viewed from a focal point related to the movement of the visitors, and located somewhere in a unidirectional line that would go around the entire room, traversing the wall at eye level. There would be two real clocks, one at the beginning and one at the end of the line. It was called *Time-Perspective Room*. The third installation was suggested by Alexius von Meinong's writings. I was fascinated by his theory of objects: "Objects remain objects and have a definitive character and definite property even if they have no existence: a gilded mountain is gilded and is a mountain, even if a similar object doesn't exist." So I started thinking about images that, no matter how realistic, are actually only mental objects. In the planned installation *Nonexistent Objects Room* of 1978 would be such images as Alice's looking glass, from Lewis Carroll, and Etienne de Condillac's sentient statue, Meinong's gilded mountain, Chuang Tzu's yellow butterfly, Rudolf Hermann Lotze's hypothetical animal, Lao Tze's infinite stick, the fourth dimension, and so on. The description of each of these abstract objects was to be printed on almost immaterial surfaces— transparent sheets of glass, and a progression of glass cubes, which were to fill the entire space as pedestals for imaginary, "nonexistent" objects.

GC: In *Blue Triangle*, 1980, from "*De More Geometrico*," the Bergsonian spirit of time is united with the atomized path of the bird and with the infinite divisibility of space and of the moment. Besides the formal and mathematical aspects of the infinitesimal, I am interested, again, in the bird's role as an image relating sky and earth, while the triangle (the form that multiplies and governs the work, as the element of fragmentation) is an indicator of harmony and of proportion. The use of the bird seems to refer both to Maréy and to Giacomo Balla, and thus to Futurism, just as the triangle of light can refer to Rosicrucian symbolism. How do you see the commingling of these figures?

LG: As an artist I have never been concerned with Rosicrucian philosophy, or with the other spiritualist philosophies of the late 19th and early 20th centuries that attribute special spiritual or mystical qualities to the triangle. Instinctively, however, I can feel the purity of that perfect geometric shape. I used it as a reflective form—"reflectivity as definition of the infinite," as George Cantor said—and I looked at it from the point of view of the divisibility of a space. Each triangle can be divided into others, which can themselves be divided into still more, always smaller triangles. And the original triangle can itself be considered a fragment of an infinite triangular form. For Balla and the Futurists, and for Maréy, movement was visualized through the representation of a sequence of images succeeding in time. My triangle subdivides and multiplies its geometric form in space as in a perspective of mirrors, a progression in which the triangular images become smaller and smaller in each succeeding reflection.

In *Minimum Discernible*, 1977, the flight of birds is used to investigate the limits of visual perception as they relate to the dynamic of time. It shows the division of movement applied to an instant of visual duration that becomes progressively shorter. The flight of birds is subjected to a continuous process of division until it reaches the "minimum discernible," the limit of our visual perception of an image.

GC: One could also read these pieces as mosaics, as an aggregate of tesserae recounting a visual and rational investigation into movement and duration.

LG: I have used the concept of mosaic to capture and break the flow of light, and to reflect and illuminate the mystery of specularity. The tesserae of the mosaic create a fragmented vision. Through their subdivision of the image, they give an effect of temporary immobility—the hieratic quality of silence and stillness. The colored tesserae, with all of their different shapes, divide the images, break and multiply the effects of light.

GC: The measure of time is the measure of light in your sundial works.

LG: Many of my works are related to the concept of time. A static object blocks time and space. The absence of movement annuls the instant of time. The sundials are static objects, but they are also instruments to measure the movement of light. Their shadows create a measure of time relative to the length of the day, to the season, to the weather. Their relativity interested me as a boundary in the continuous flow of time, in which the present, the past, and the future become simultaneous in a continuous present related to the light of day.

GC: Beginning in 1983, your research passed from the use of photography and linear or sequential, always two-dimensional montage (from *Endless Dialogue* through *Blue Triangle*) to complex constructions and assemblage structures that present themselves as wall sculptures. Here too there is the choice of the labyrinth, but a labyrinth in which the objects determine the voyage and the route, the analogies and the oppositions. The memory of Futurism has been left behind, and the passage seems to be toward a "metaphysical" objectification, toward a concrete memory of your history or of your culture.

LG: The wall sculptures embody a plurality of linguistic means, through the use of a large number of different media and objects. This continuous variation of materials creates a flow of images based on a matrix of the European past—a cultural link with different historical concepts and territories, passing from one to the next through the same basic notions as in my preceding works, as if in a labyrinth of memories and objects.

In the wall sculptures of 1985, the process is a mental approach in which objects become instruments or tools to clarify a concept. The work assumes a dialectical quality; it is a dialogue between objects and forms, and among a variety of different materials, each with its own linguistic meaning. Some works are painted in gold, which reflects light and increases the sense of three-dimensionality. Others contain mosaic or marble, with all their art-historical associations. They represent different art-historical meanings and periods, taken out of their usual context to be focused in a new one. Many references coexist in the same piece: *Apollinaire's Secret*, for example, contains a little *stile nuovo* volume of Dante, and a bronze egg that refers to Piero della Francesca's Urbino fresco, but the structure that holds these objects is a Cubist tondo. A representation of the "one and his double" and the "one and the many" is found in *Parmenides's Moon*.

In *Classical Symmetry* I wanted to represent the law of symmetry and the classical, single-viewpoint, Renaissance perspective in opposition to the fourth-dimensional perspective that is a stratification of different levels of time and variable viewpoints in

space. Some of the objects within these wall sculptures are usable, such as the hourglass that can be turned over, or a little volume that can be taken out and read. The concept of reflectivity is represented in *Borromini's Violin*, which contains a bronze violin—an object Baroque in form—and its double, an identical but tiny violin hidden in the central oval. A Bach rondo, a Baroque, repetitive mathematical structure, is etched in a bronze tablet in the same work.

GC: To conclude. In 1989, the date of this interview, your work and your life revolve around New York. What relationships do you see between the landscape in which you initially moved, the city of Rome, and your new panorama? The question specifically concerns your most recent work, which has a strong Baroque component, almost a plastic compensation for American linearity.

LG: In opposition to the univocal character of contemporary art, I wanted to explore the Baroque world of diversity and its elaborated form. Though Baroque forms appear in the wall sculptures (which I called "The Baroque Series"), Cubist and classical forms do as well. The wall sculptures, taken together, are a kind of diary of multiple interests and influences. They represent a plurality of meanings through an elaboration of many different forms. In this latter sense, I consider these works connected to the Baroque visual experience. They are signals transmitted by a culture of the past, of another place and time, to create confrontation and reaction. They are an arena in which different elements coexist in a relationship based on mimesis and conflict. I like to recycle art objects and meanings—different things become the same thing. The Baroque cupola of a Roman church or the spire of a New York skyscraper can be seen as similar symbols in different contexts and cultures. I am interested in a changing process through which a unity of concepts can be achieved.

Following pages:
Classical Symmetry *(detail),*
1985

A Selection of Works,
with Notes by the Artist

Variable Paintings

I liked the thought of a painting that didn't always look the same. I was interested in exploring the idea of variability, in making a painting that allowed viewers to change the image as they liked—for a few minutes, a few hours, a few months, or more. In each variation the painting can be read in a different way.

Each painting has two or more sliding panels of painted canvas and colored Plexiglas that can be moved by the viewer to create different superimpositions and to reveal previously hidden parts of the work. In some of them, the color of a section of the image can be altered by shading it with a different-colored transparent panel. This creates the possibility of many variations in the same painting. In several works, a revolving Plexiglas disk provides an even greater range of possibilities.

Right and following pages:
Transparent Door *(details), 1965*
Acrylic on canvas, Plexiglas,
sliding panel
65 × 155 × 4 inches
(165 × 394 × 10 cm)
The sliding panel is made of
fluorescent-yellow Plexiglas. As
the viewer moves it across the
background images, it changes
their colors.

Right and following pages:
Geometric Landscape, *1966*
Acrylic on canvas, collage,
Plexiglas, sliding panel
79 × 88 × 4 inches
(200 × 224 × 10 cm) closed;
80 × 120 × 4 inches
(200 × 300 × 10 cm) open.
The sliding panels in two
different positions.

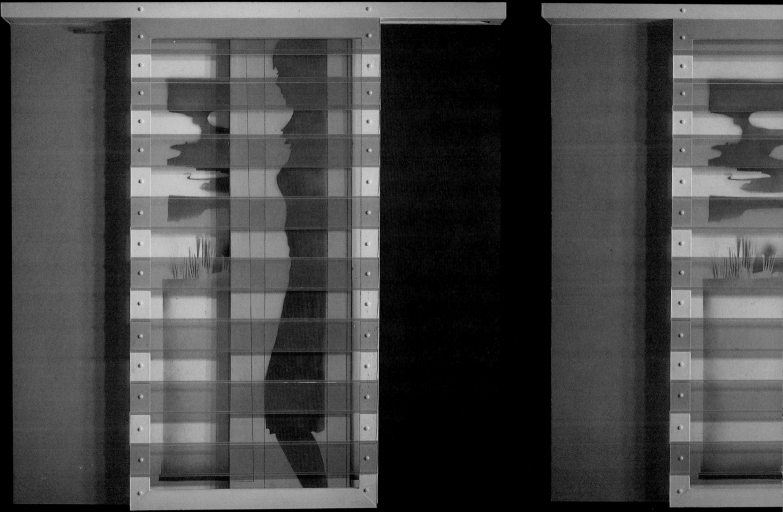

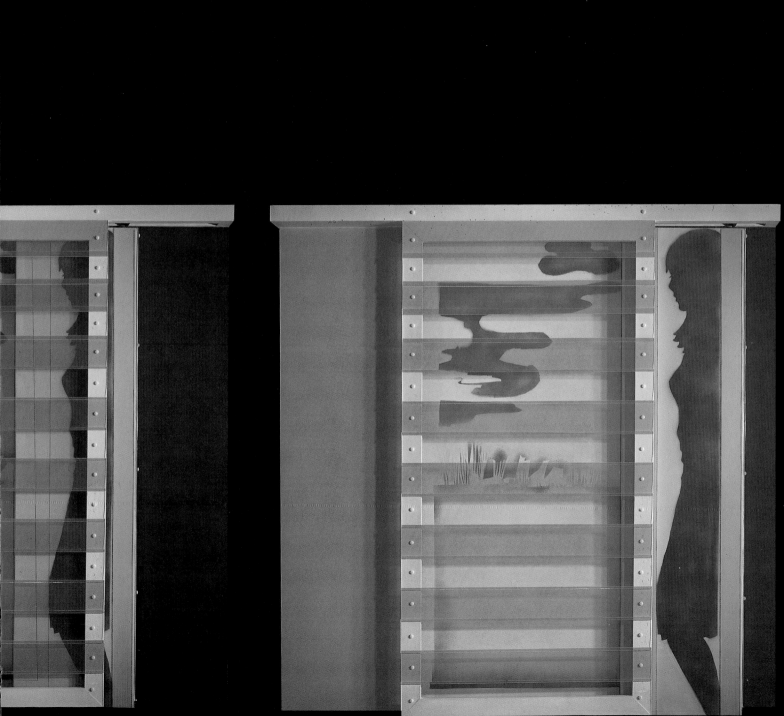

Seascape, *1966*
Acrylic on canvas, Plexiglas,
sliding panels containing cast-
Plexiglas clouds
38 × 49 × 4 inches
(96.5 × 124 × 10 cm)
Left, with panels open;
right, with panels closed.

East Window, *1966*
Acrylic on canvas, Plexiglas,
sliding panels containing cast-
Plexiglas clouds
66 × 64 × 6 inches
(168 × 162.5 × 15 cm)
Collection Mrs. Fernanda
Bonino, New York
Three configurations of the
same work.

Neon Paintings

In this next body of work, the Plexiglas, panels, and disks of the "Variable Paintings" remained, but neon, metal, and wood were added, moving the works out from the wall into space.

Sections of the pieces are covered with panels of textured plastic, usually ribbed, which distort and obscure the details, creating an illusory effect of depth and perspective. The internal panels are designed to slide, so that the arrangement of the figures can be altered at will.

Actually not very deep, these works create the effect of night space, in which the shadows of people move mysteriously on unknown errands, coming and going in an illusory urban environment of glowing neon signs and glancing reflections.

Left:
Installation in the "Young
Italians" exhibition at the
Institute of Contemporary Art,
Boston, 1968, with East Village
(left) and Subway

Below:
East Village, *1967*
Acrylic on canvas, neon,
Plexiglas, galvanized
aluminum
63½ × 66 × 8¾ inches
(163 × 167 × 22 cm)

Booth, *1967*
Neon, Plexiglas, enamel on
aluminum, sliding panel
68 × 42 × 10 inches
(173 × 106 × 25 cm)
Illuminated from the outside.
The figure within slides on a
movable panel.

Booth, *1967*
Neon, Plexiglas, enamel on
aluminum, sliding panel
68 × 42 × 10 inches
(173 × 106 × 25 cm)
Illuminated from the outside.
The figure within slides on a
movable panel.

Booth, *1967*
By the light of its own neon.

Top Floor, *1967*
Neon, Plexiglas, aluminum
68 × 55 × 9 inches
(173 × 140 × 22 cm)
Collection Ludwig, Neue
Galerie, Aachen

Below:
Top Floor, *1967*

Following pages:
St. Marks Place *(detail), 1967*
Neon, Plexiglas, aluminum,
wood, sliding panels
68 × 75 × 10 inches
(173 × 190 × 25 cm)
Both illuminated by their own
neon.

Subway, *1967*
Neon, Plexiglas, aluminum,
sliding panel
66 × 41½ × 8¾ inches
(167 × 103 × 22 cm)

Subway, *1967*
The figure within slides.

470, Angolare, *1967*
Neon, Plexiglas, aluminum
68½ × 42 × 10 inches
(174 × 106 × 25 cm)
Collection Mr. and Mrs. Baum,
Wuppertal

470, Angolare *(detail), 1967,*
installed with Sunset Lamp,
1967
Neon, Plexiglas, steel
88½ × 12 × 12 inches
(225 × 30 × 30 cm)

Racing Car Room

I loved Lotus formula-one cars, and I dreamed of seeing dozens of them all together in one room. So I set Plexiglas cutouts of them in boxes lit from the inside with neon, then multiplied them by installing them on a shiny aluminum base. Having made the reflecting floor, I also made a ceiling, *Blue*, to create an entire environment.

Right:
Model Car Racing *(detail), 1967*
Five neon, Plexiglas, and
aluminum boxes on a reflecting
aluminum base. The largest
box: 31½ × 67 × 5 inches
(80 × 170 × 13 cm). The base:
78 × 100 × 4 inches
(200 × 250 × 10 cm)
Installation view at the Galerie
E. M. Thelen, Essen, 1968

Following four pages:
Model Car Racing *(details),*
1967, and, on the ceiling in the
first photograph, Blue, *1967*
Neon, Plexiglas, aluminum
7 × 66 × 47 inches
(17 × 168 × 120 cm)
Installation views at the Galerie
E. M. Thelen, Essen, 1968

Natural Elements—A Space of Fog

In 1968, I worked with natural elements and phenomena such as fog, water, wind, air, rainbows, and other effects of light. Artificially reproduced in an enclosed space, such properties of the outer environment alter its psychological structure by their presence.

Un Area di Nebbia (A Space of Fog) is the first of these projects. A dense fog, artificially created by a hidden machine, filled an enclosed space, creating the illusion of the outdoors. The fog was pierced by the cool light of *Antinebbia*, or antifog lights—spirals of neon in gradations of color from blue to white, set in six transparent structures. The fog became a plastic form, defining the space and its mood, hiding both viewers and the neon spirals, diffusing their light.

Right:
Un Area di Nebbia
(A Space of Fog), 1968
Artificial fog, spiral neon
tubing, Plexiglas, steel
Installation view at the
Marlborough Gallery, Rome,
1969

Un Area di Nebbia, *1968*
Installation view, 1969

Left and below:
Antinebbia *(Antifog), 1968*
Spiral neon tubing, Plexiglas,
steel
Six pieces, each 118½ × 12 × 12
inches (300 × 30 × 30 cm)
One piece, collection of the
Galleria Nazionale d'Arte
Moderna, Rome; another,
Johnssen Collection, Essen;
others, collection of the artist.
Installation views outdoors in
Rome, 1968

Below and following pages:
Antinebbia, *1968*

91

Natural Elements—Refraction

During a trip to Africa in 1968, I walked along the
shore of Lake Chad. The water by the sand dunes was
calm and shallow, and the sunlight glancing off its
surface made me want to try an experiment in
refraction. Using the stems of saplings growing along
the shore, I carried out a practical test. I set them in
the lake so that they would float at different angles,
creating an unusual demonstration of the phenomenon
of refraction. Later, I worked on the same idea for an
indoor project, made with thin, weighted aluminum
tubes floating at oblique angles to the surface of the
water in four cylindrical tanks. At the intersection of
tube and water, the light created the refraction effect.
Since the tubes were free-floating, their reflections
and refractions constantly changed.

Right:
Lake Chad

97

Natural Elements—Rain Room

A natural phenomenon—drops of rain—was artificially recreated in an enclosed environment. A pipe filled with water was suspended from the ceiling. From small holes at different points in the pipe, drops of water fell continuously into a large round basin of water. Since this basin was sunk into a raised floor, the water level was the same as the surrounding plane. The falling drops made different sounds and formed a constant series of concentric ripples. There was the sensation of listening to the rhythmic sound of the rain.

Right and following four pages:
Drops of Water (details), 1968
Water, white fiberglass basin,
white metal pipe
Basin: 78 inches diam., 10
inches deep (200 cm diam.,
25 cm deep); pipe: 220 inches
long, 2 inches diam. (564 cm
long, 5 cm diam.)
Installation views in the "Earth
Air Fire Water: Elements of
Art" exhibition at the Museum
of Fine Arts, Boston, 1971

Natural Elements—Wind

While traveling in various countries I began to film images of wind speeds and their effects. I also took measurements in the desert and on the shores of the ocean, studying both natural movements of air—the wind blowing unchecked over sand, sea, and fields, or obstructed and channeled by the trees of a forest or the walls of a big city—and those produced mechanically, for example by the rotors of a helicopter. These experiments are shown in a 16-mm film, *Wind Speed 40 Knots*. The same year, using wind machines, I reproduced the effects of this 40-knot blow indoors, in a gallery space in Rome.

Wind Speed 40 Knots *(details)*,
1968
Black and white film in 16 mm,
15 minutes

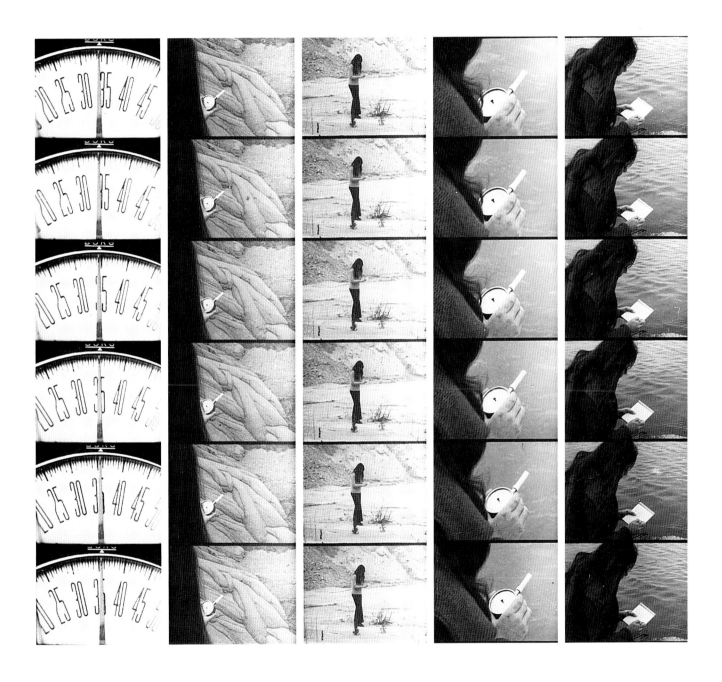

Natural Elements—Wind Room

A semidark room was divided by a screen made of black-painted wooden slats. Hidden behind it, several theatrical fans artificially reproduced a wind of about 40 knots, which blew through the screen and invaded the rest of the space. Entering the room, one was enveloped by this continuous wind, a totally unexpected natural element in the enclosed space, creating different reactions and sensations in each visitor.

Above and right:
Wind Speed 40 Knots, *1968*
Environment of black-painted
wood and wind machines
Installation views at the Galleria
La Tartaruga, Rome, 1968

Natural Elements—Air Room

A very thin thread of bright white light was drawn in neon along the perimeter edges—the junctures of floor, walls, and ceiling—of an exactly cubic room painted in fluorescent white. The light was brilliant enough that it almost seemed to acquire a dimension of density, so that upon entering the space one had the sensation, visual and almost tactile, of a contained volume of air.

Left and below:
Volume of Air, *1968*
Fluorescent-white-painted wood
walls, white ceiling, white floor,
white neon tubes
Room: 180 × 180 × 180 inches
(450 × 450 × 450 cm); neon
tubes: ½ inch diam. (1.3 cm
diam.)
Installation views in the "Nuovi
Materiali, Nuove Tecniche"
exhibition in Caorle, Venezia,
1969

Natural Elements—Stars
A pinpoint hole in each of four aluminum sheets diffracts a bright light behind it, making a sparkle effect like a star.

Stars, *1968*
Galvanized aluminum, Osram
lamps
Four parts, each 20 × 20 × 4
inches (50 × 50 × 10 cm)

Natural Elements—Star Room

A space was divided by a wall of lead hiding high-intensity pinpoint lights that burned at 350 degrees centigrade. The lights were programmed to go on one by one, melting the lead in 25 seconds, always at different points of the wall. A brilliant ray of light burst from the tiny holes made by the melting process. The entire lead wall glowed with this sprinkling of luminous stars created by the diffraction of the intense light.

Light Melting Time *(detail),*
1968
Lead sheet, Osram lamps
Lead: 117 × 98 inches
(300 × 250 cm); 64 lamps
Installation view at the Galleria
del Naviglio, Milan, 1970

Light Melting Time, *1968*
Installation view, 1970

Light Melting Time, *1968*
Installation view, 1970

Light Melting Time, *1968*
Installation view, 1970

Natural Elements—Rainbow

A closed square space in semidarkness. A thin ray of light pierced four hidden prisms, recreating the colors of the solar spectrum. Every wall was traversed by a luminous horizontal line in the colors of the rainbow.

Rainbow, *1968*
Prisms, light
Installation view

Natural Elements—Whirlpool Room

A film projector was concealed in the ceiling of a
circular space built specifically for the project. The
image of a whirlpool was continuously projected onto
the floor, completely covering it. Entering the space,
one had the sensation of being at the whirlpool's
center. The continuous motion and the changing color
had a real intensity.

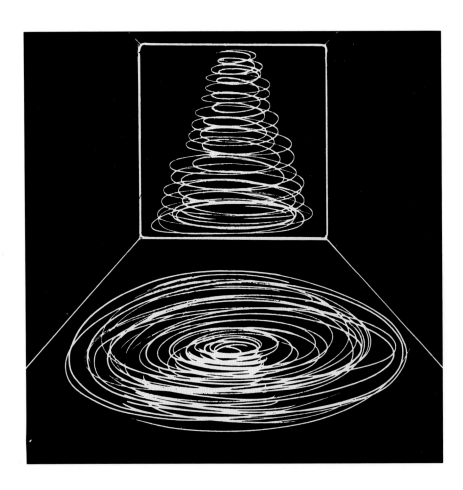

Preceding page:
Whirlpool Room Drawing, *1969*
A plan proposing a mirrored
wall to reflect the image
projected on the floor.

Below and following pages:
Whirlpool *(details), 1969*
Color film in 16 mm

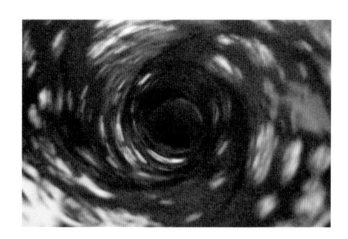

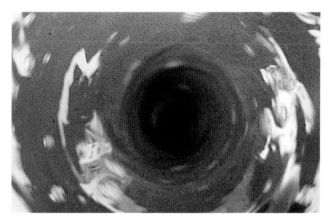

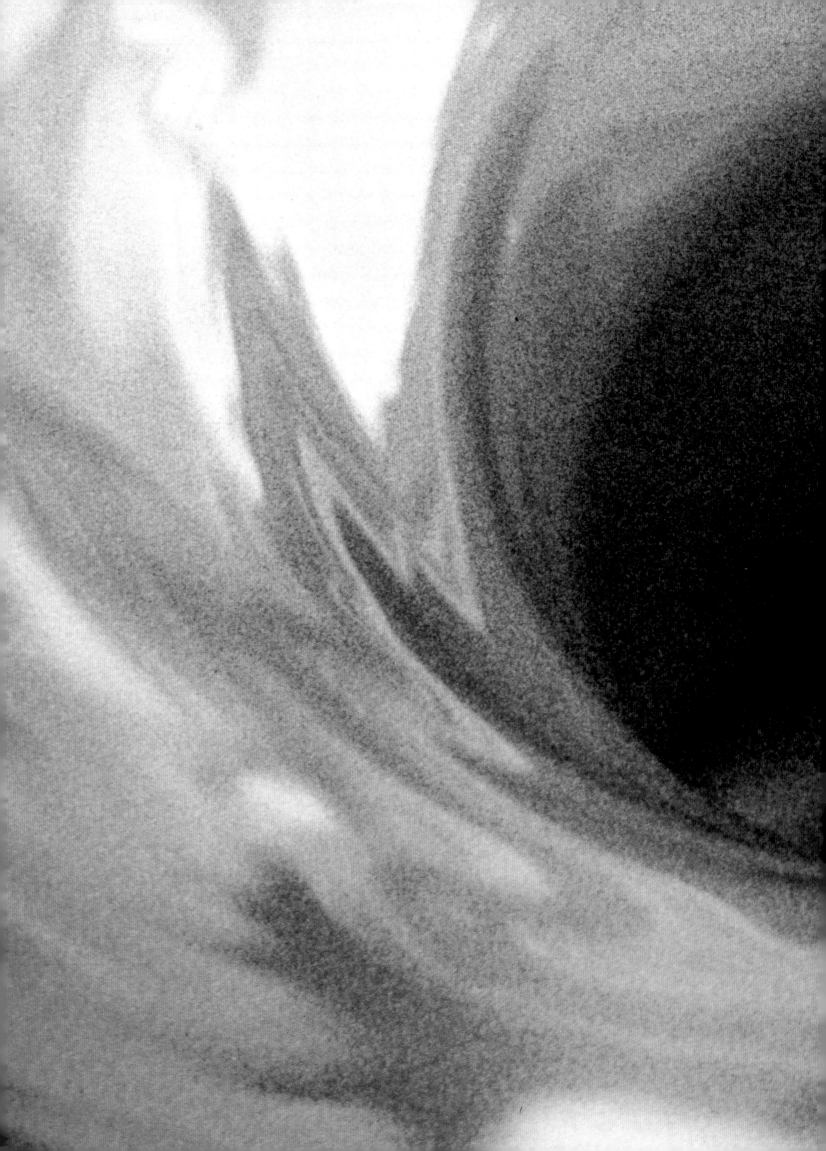

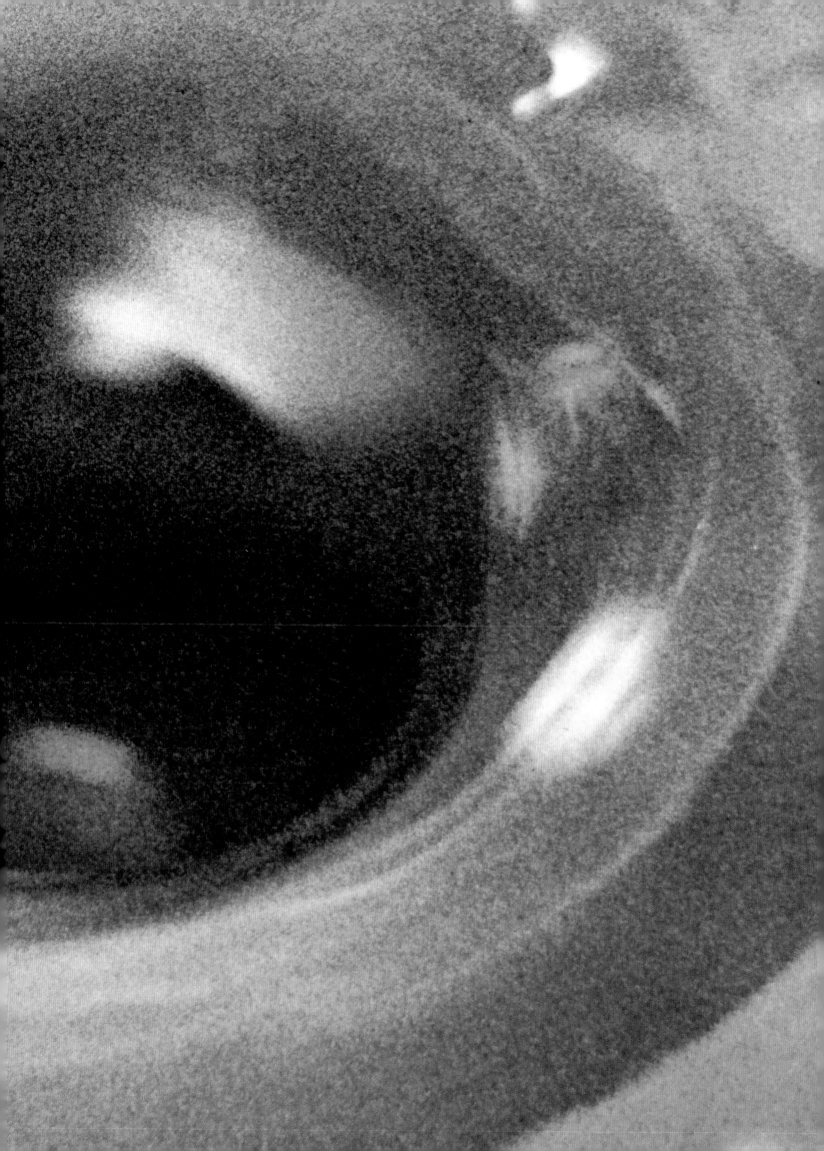

Distillations

This group of works was related to my travels in parts of the world where the symbols and rituals of primitive cultures, though disappearing, were still alive. I called the works "Distillations": analyses of sensations and personal reactions to different environments, cultural contexts, and ethnic groups. Some of them were related to my experiences of the philosophies of different cultures, and had a meditative quality.

In *The Measuring of Time*, the counting of grains of sand in the desert, as an instrument of measure, represented an infinite action beyond time. This endless, repetitive gesture was emphasized in a film, which was shot in a single spiral sequence, beginning with a close-up of the hands counting the grains of sand and expanding outward to reveal the figure performing the action. Then the camera moved in again, the spiral motion reconstricting until it returned to the detail of the hands, concluding the sequence.

The Measuring of Time
(details), 1969
Two versions: black and white
film in 16 mm, color videotape

128

Distillations—3 Months of Looking

While I was traveling for three months in 1970, I analyzed my feelings and reactions on experiencing the new environments, and on watching and observing objects and elements changing under different natural conditions. Physical sensations and emotions such as fear or pain, or visual perceptions of varieties and similarities in color, movement, and shape, were the subject of the work, which was

I LOOK AT VARIETY IN PLANTS

RAW DATA:

I walk in an orchid plantation and look at their varieties, qualities and colors.
There are other plants - some mango-trees. I look intently at their leaves and fruit, some over-mature ones have fallen down and broken open.

TITLE: Sameness in colors

PROPOSITION:

To find a color similarity in two different plants under the same conditions of light and at the same time of day. The similarity can be found in either the leaves, the flowers or the fruit of the two plants.

CONDITIONS FOR THE EXPERIMENT:

1. Find oneself in an orchid plantation at the time of day when the light is most intense
2. It is necessary to have some mango-trees in the same plantation
3. Be there in the period of the year when the orchids are in flower
4. Be there in the period of the year when the mangos are mature
5. Examine the different plants at the same hour and in the same light

INSTRUCTIONS:

1. Look carefully at the color of the different orchids
2. Select the most intense color
3. Look carefully at the color of the mango-leaves (especially the new ones)
4. Select the lightest green
5. Once the colors are selected, find the equivalent of one in the other plant and vice versa.

NOTES:

A) I found that the orchid with the most intense color has the same color as the pulp of ripe mango.
B) I found that the lightest green of new mango leaves is the same green as that of the veining of the orchid.

PLACE: Mindanao
       Sulu Islands
DATE : July 13, 1970
TIME : 12 noon

I LOOK AT HOW PALMS MOVE

RAW DATA:

I look at palms and other trees moving, without time limits. Some palms move very slowly, the movement of other trees is different. With the same gust of wind, each tree has a different time of response; the top of each tree is the part that moves more quickly, the leaves on the central branches more slowly. The outside leaves turn in every direction even though the wind blows in only one direction. If leaves and fruit fall down, coconuts fall the most frequently. In some trees the leaves fall first, in the breadfruit tree the flowers fall first, in the banana tree the leaves only move, in the frangipane tree only the small branches at the top (where the flowers are) break and fall. The most rapid movement is that of the palm, and includes also the flexible trunk which bends. After each gust of wind the tree which straightens the soonest is the palm, but that which stops the first is the frangipane; the ones whose leaves continue to move the longest are the breadfruit and the pandanus. Each leaf moves with a different sound. Palm trees give a hissing sound, other trees a drier one; those with smaller leaves a more rapid and metallic sound. The frangipane trees do not have leaves, only branches and flowers, and give a light sound, that of the impact of the wind against the branches, a barely audible sound. The deepest sound is that of the pandanus tree.

TITLE: Indeterminacy

CONDITIONS FOR THE EXPERIMENT:

1. An area with trees and various kinds of vegetation
2. Silence
3. Solitude
4. Gusts of wind

INSTRUCTIONS:

1. Select a place where it is possible to see more than one kind of tree at the same time
2. Observe the behavior of each tree during and after each gust of wind
3. First watch one tree at a time, note the differences; try to look at all of them together during the same gust
4. Going close to each tree, listen to the sound it makes.

NOTES:

I do not want to establish anything precise: only observe without time limits.

PLACE: Maupiti
       Leeward Islands
DATE : August 23, 1970
TIME : 3 p. m.

Distillations: 3 Months of Looking (details), 1970
Book, Macerata: Edizione Artestudio

divided into eight parts: "I look at variety in plants—Mindanao, Sulu Islands"; "I look at how palms move—Maupiti, Leeward Islands"; "I look at fire—Chad Desert"; "I look at how the ocean moves—Rangiroa"; "I look at the horizon—Niger Desert"; "I look at a lava flow—Tanna Volcano, New Hebrides"; "I look at the sun—Manihi, Tuamotu Atolls," and "I look at water—Raiatea, Leeward Islands."

I LOOK AT FIRE

RAW DATA:

We are in the desert at night. There is a wind, it is cold and we have lighted a fire. I watch the color of the flames to establish the direction of the wind: the flames change color according to their movement. Looking intently only at the color changes and their frequency, I try to establish the force and the direction of the wind.

PLACE: Tchad desert
DATE : September 22, 1970
TIME : 11 p. m.

TITLE: Difference in colors

PROPOSITION:

Establish the force and direction of the wind by the color changes in the flames of a lighted fire at night. On the basis of these data, calculate in how much time the wind will consume the fire.

CONDITIONS FOR THE EXPERIMENT:

1. A lighted fire in the open at night
2. A strong wind of at least 20 miles per hour

INSTRUCTIONS:

1. Establish an initial base point: a given gradation of color corresponds to a given movement of the flames in a given direction
2. Watch only the color of the flames
3. From the variations in color, calculate the number of times a color repeats itself and how frequently
4. From the frequency with which a color is repeated (knowing already to what movement and, therefore, to what direction of the wind it corresponds) establish the force of the wind
5. Calculate the time in which the fire will be consumed in relation to the quantity of combustible material.

EQUATION: V = Wind velocity
T = Time necessary to consume the fire
t = Duration of each gust of wind
Q = Quantity of combustible material (wood)

$$\frac{Q}{t \cdot V} = T$$

I LOOK AT HOW THE OCEAN MOVES

RAW DATA:

I look at the ocean moving, without time limits, how the waves move, when, which are larger, which are smaller, where and at what intervals big waves form, in which fishes can be seen in transparency, in which only foam, which come further up the sand, which are shortest, at what distance from one another they break, which give the deepest sound, which leave debris on the sand, which seaweed, which fish

PLACE: Rangiroa
DATE : August 25, 1970
TIME : 5 p. m.

TITLE: Indeterminacy

CONDITIONS FOR THE EXPERIMENT:

1. The ocean, not completely calm
2. Silence
3. Solitude
4. Any day after a storm, when there are algae and debris in the water

INSTRUCTIONS:

1. To look at the ocean until the sunset
2. Not to stand still in one place, but to walk along the edge of the water
3. Not to become distracted by the surrounding scenery

NOTES:

I do not want to establish anything precise: only observe without any time limits.

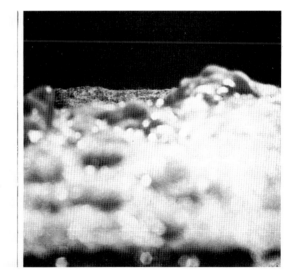

Distillations—Choice and Choosing 16 from 5000
The material of this book is a selection of groups of
images from 5,000 traveling photographs. They were
taken with several different lenses, at different times,
under different conditions, during several separate
journeys to countries containing different ethnic
groups and "primitive" cultures. The images I chose
for the work were related by similarities of form,
subject matter, and other visual affinities. After
sorting them into 16 classes, I restructured them into
single "image symbols," rephotographing each group
with the same lens, in the same conditions of time,
light, and environment, to give them a psychological
and visual unity.

Distillations: Choice and
Choosing 16 from 5000 *(details),*
1970
Book, Macerata: Edizione
Artestudio
"Mudmen." Left: as first
photographed; right: the
photographs reshot.

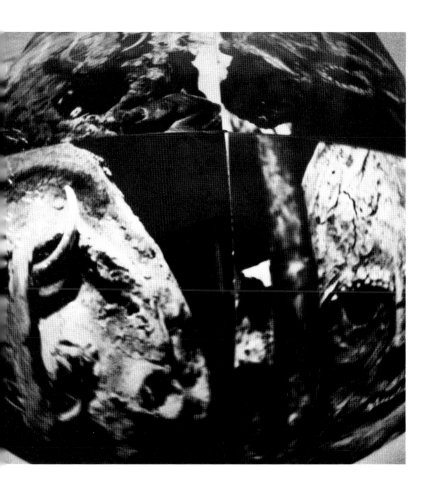

Distillations: Choice and
Choosing 16 from 5000 *(details)*,
1970
*"People." Left: the images as
they were shot—with different
lenses, under different
conditions, in different places,
and at different times; right: the
images reshot with one lens, at
the same place, at the same
time.*

Distillations: Choice and
Choosing 16 from 5000 *(details)*,
1970
"*Reflections.*"

Distillations: Choice and
Choosing 16 from 5000 *(details)*,
1970
"Birdmen."

Equilibrium—To Carlotta Grisi
This project from 1971 is about gravity, equilibrium, and dance. It consists of the drawings for a group of environments inspired by the 19th-century dancer Carlotta Grisi.

NEW PAS DE QUATRE, BY MDLLES. TAGLIONI, C. GRI

SMYTH

GRAHN, AND CERITO, AT HER MAJESTY'S THEATRE.

Below and right:
Equilibrium: To Carlotta Grisi—
Pas de Quatre, *1971*
*Five drawings for an
environment
From an image of the* pas de
quatre *movement in a 19th-
century ballet.*

*Four spheres suspended from
flexible wires move in space on
four different trajectories.
Every 30 seconds, one of them
stops; remaining motionless at
a nonperpendicular angle to the
ground, it seems to defy gravity.
Then it resumes its movement.
All the spheres move and stop
alternately, always at different
angles.*

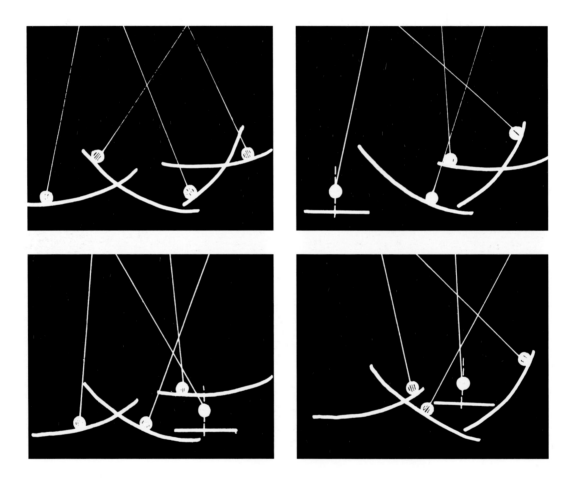

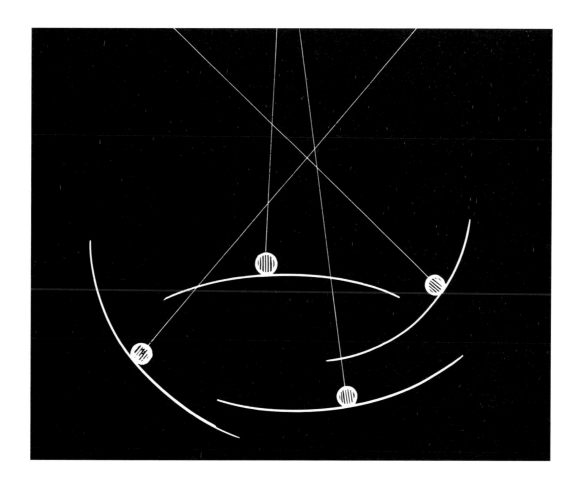

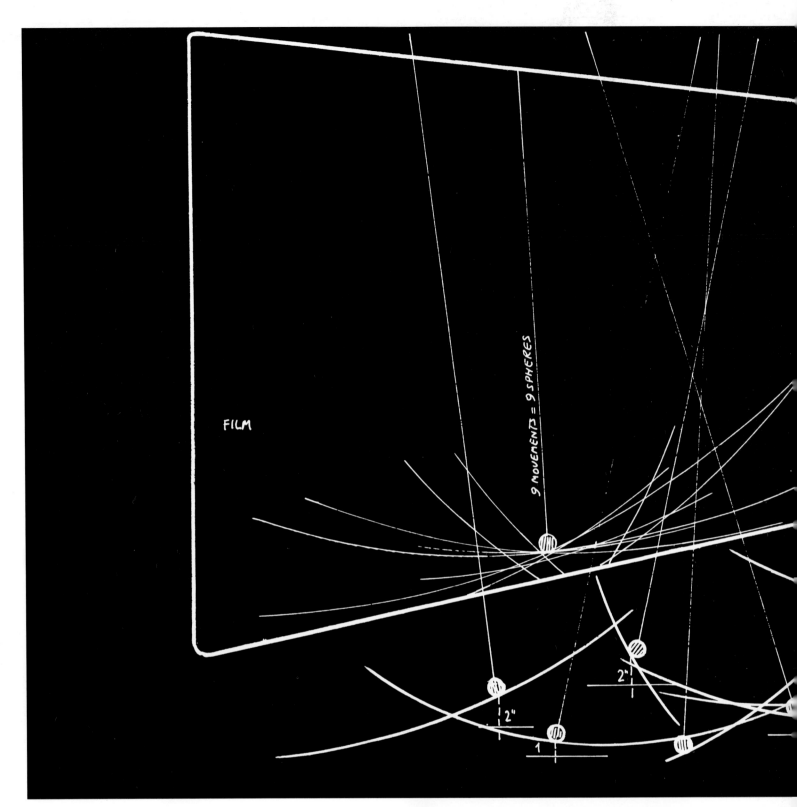

FILM

9 MOVEMENTS = 9 SPHERES

UNO

VI

2"

VII

2"

VIII

1

LA PÉRI, 1843. CARLOTTA GRISI ET LUCIEN PETIPA

144

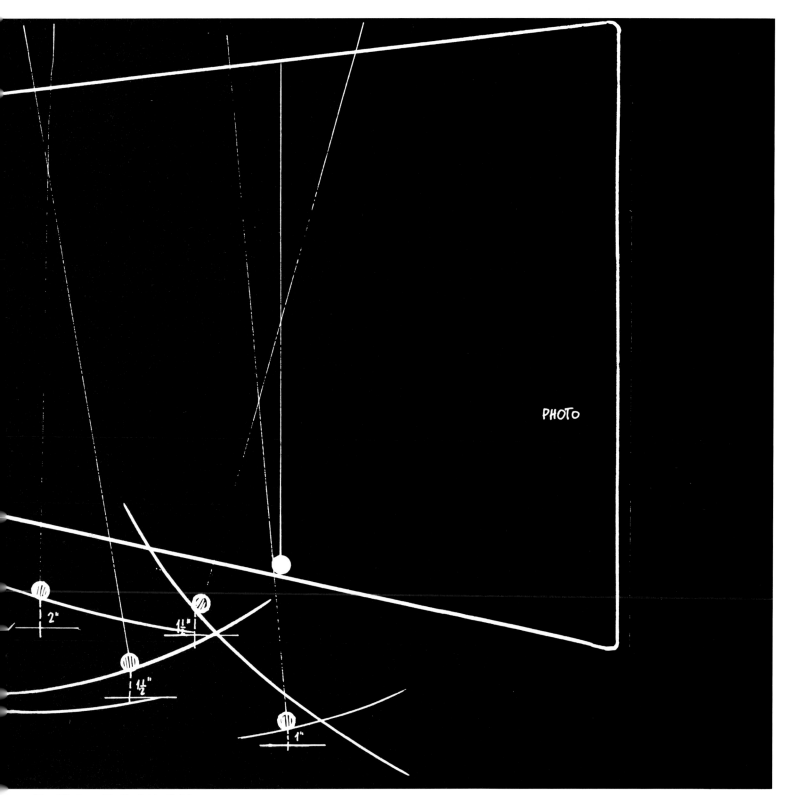

PHOTO

Equilibrium: To Carlotta Grisi—
Beyond Gravity, *1971*
Drawing for an environment
From an image of the ballet La
Peri, *1843, with Carlotta Grisi*
and Lucien Petipa.

Nine spheres swing through
space on wires. They suddenly
stop, at a variety of angles to the
perpendicular. Next, two
projections appear on facing
walls: a still photograph of a
sphere hanging on a
perpendicular wire, and a film
of a sphere moving through all
the different angles established
by the nine objects in the space.
After about a minute, the
projections end, and the spheres
resume their movement.

Equilibrium: To Carlotta Grisi—
Gravity and a Perfect Right
Angle, *1971*
Drawing for an environment
This and the following piece are
from an image of Carlotta Grisi
dancing in La Peri.

Two spheres hanging on wires
from the center of the ceiling
swing past each other across the
room. One and a half inches
from the walls, they stop in
space for 30 seconds, at 45
degrees to the vertical surface.
Then they resume their
movement. Glass panels
running inward from the side
walls form transparent wings
between the swinging spheres
and the spectator.

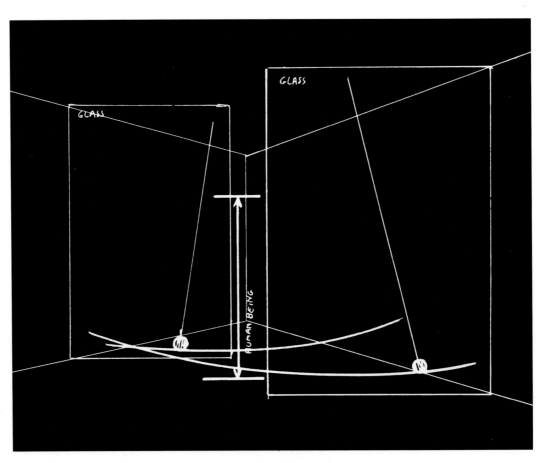

146

Equilibrium: To Carlotta Grisi—
Diagonal Division of Space
*Four drawings for an
environment*

*Four steel rods, five feet long
and a quarter inch in diameter,
project in from the centers of the
four vertical sides of a ten-foot
cube. Each rod makes two
complete semicircular
movements (a horizontal and a
vertical one). The movements of
the rods are synchronized so
that they never meet at the
center of the cube.*

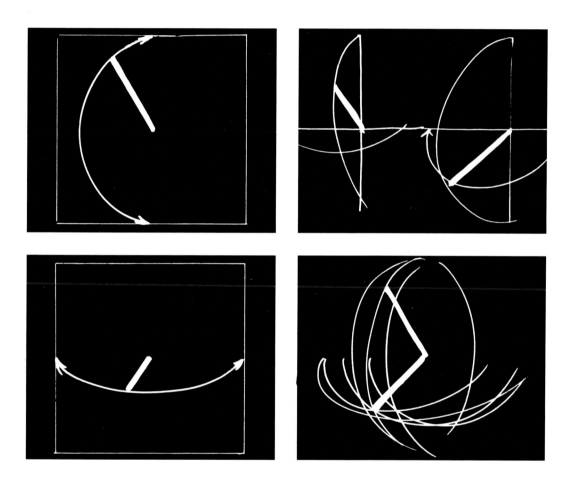

Sounds

Two cassettes contain a tape recording, made with a hypersensitive microphone, revealing similarities and minimal differences in various sounds: the random movement of ants; the expanding fibers of a tree; the aural permutations of a series of objects falling onto a series of surfaces; the sounds made by an element heard in different quantities at the same time (the waves of the ocean mixed with the falling of drops of water).

Above:
Sounds, *1971*
Two cassette tapes, 15 minutes
each side

Right:
Sounds, *1971*
"Tree" (side two). A powerful
microphone inserted in the tree
records the noises of the flowing
lymph and of the expanding
fibers.

Following pages:
Sounds, *1971*
"Ten Stones" (side one). Ordered
by weight from lightest to
heaviest, the stones are dropped
from a fixed height onto a
surface of asphalt. The sequence
is repeated on surfaces of metal,
rubber, glass, wood, water,
sand, gravel, mud, and coal.

Variations

In the "Variations," I used a finite number of stones, different in size, shape, and color, to realize an open series of combinations, giving a mental order to the natural order of things. This suggested a kind of analogy between the structure of nature used as a language of art, and an investigation of reality based on the various forms it can achieve if related to space. In other works of this group, similar implications were related to time and its serial order, to the symbolic values of such objects as coins, and to the visual values of colors.

From One to Four Pebbles
(details), 1972
Two versions: color videotape,
color film in 16 mm
Castelli-Sonnabend Tapes and
Films, New York
Every possible permutation in
the arrangement of four pebbles
in the same space, including
groups of one, two, and three, as
well as the entire set.

Preceding pages and below:
Pebbles *(details), 1973*
150 color photographs mounted
on board
Each photograph 3⅛ × 5¼
inches (8 × 13.3 cm)
Collection Leo Castelli,
New York
Every possible permutation in
the arrangement of a group of
five pebbles.

Pebbles, *1973*
Installation view in the
"Thirtieth Anniversary Show—
The First Fifteen Years: Part 2,"
Leo Castelli Greene Street
Gallery, New York, 1987

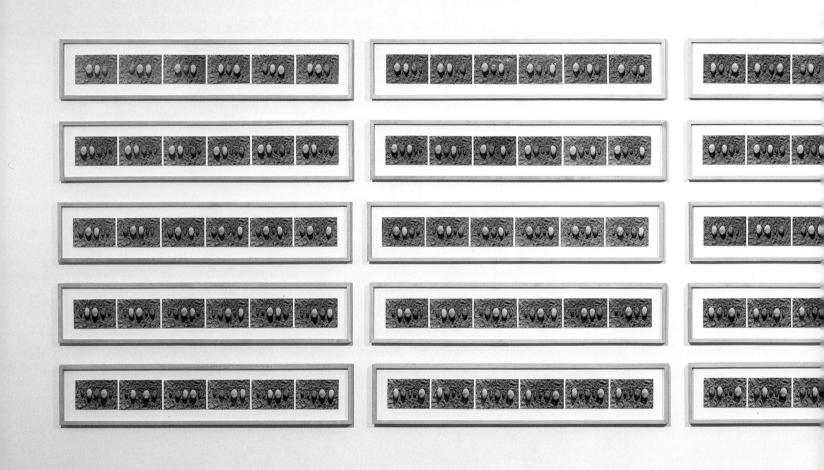

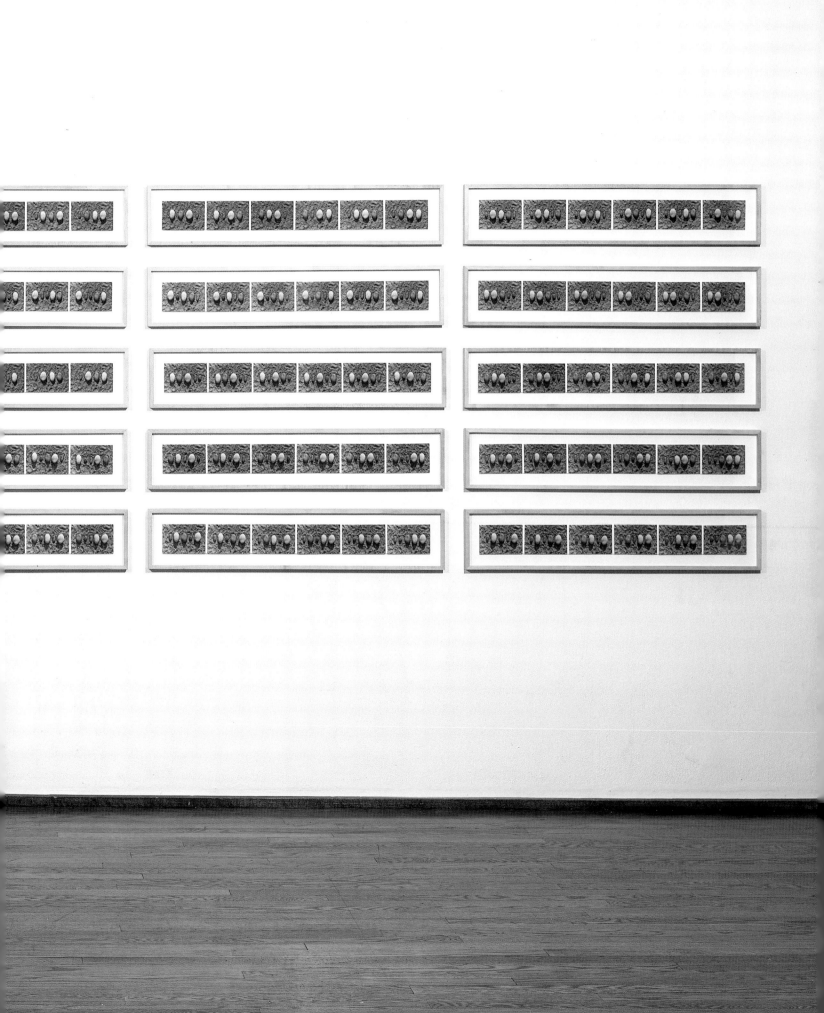

Variations—Stripes

Stripes is a work about color, specifically every possible different juxtaposition of six colors: yellow, red, blue, orange, green, and violet. The 720 juxtapositions are executed on scrolls of Japanese canvas; the first contains the plan of the various combinations, and the scrolls that follow, the permutations of every color in relation to the other five colors.

Below:
Stripes *(detail), 1974*
Ink on 13 canvas scrolls
Each scroll 119 × 13¼ inches
(302 × 34 cm)

Following pages:
Stripes, *1974*
Installation view at the Van
Abbemuseum, Eindhoven, 1976

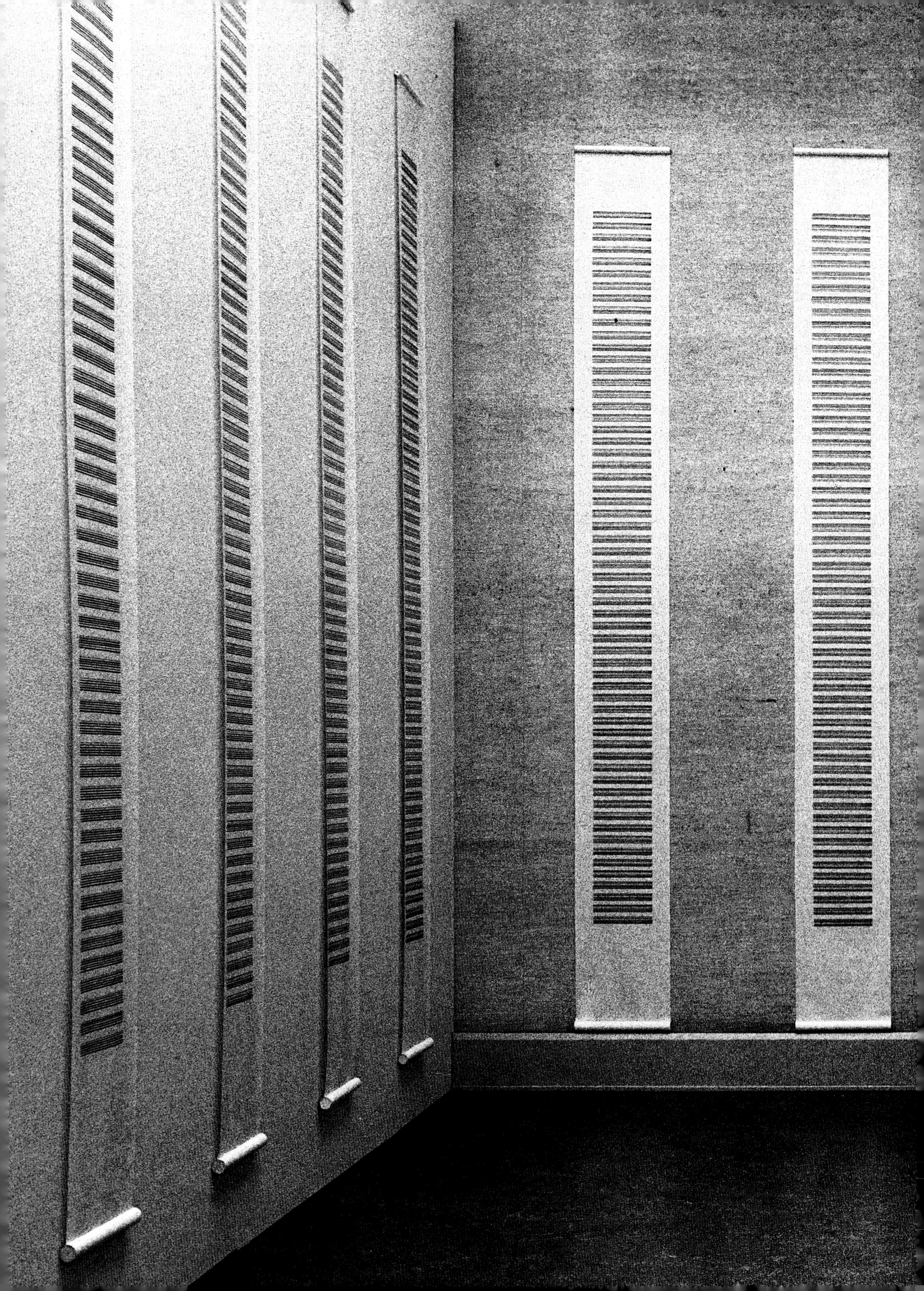

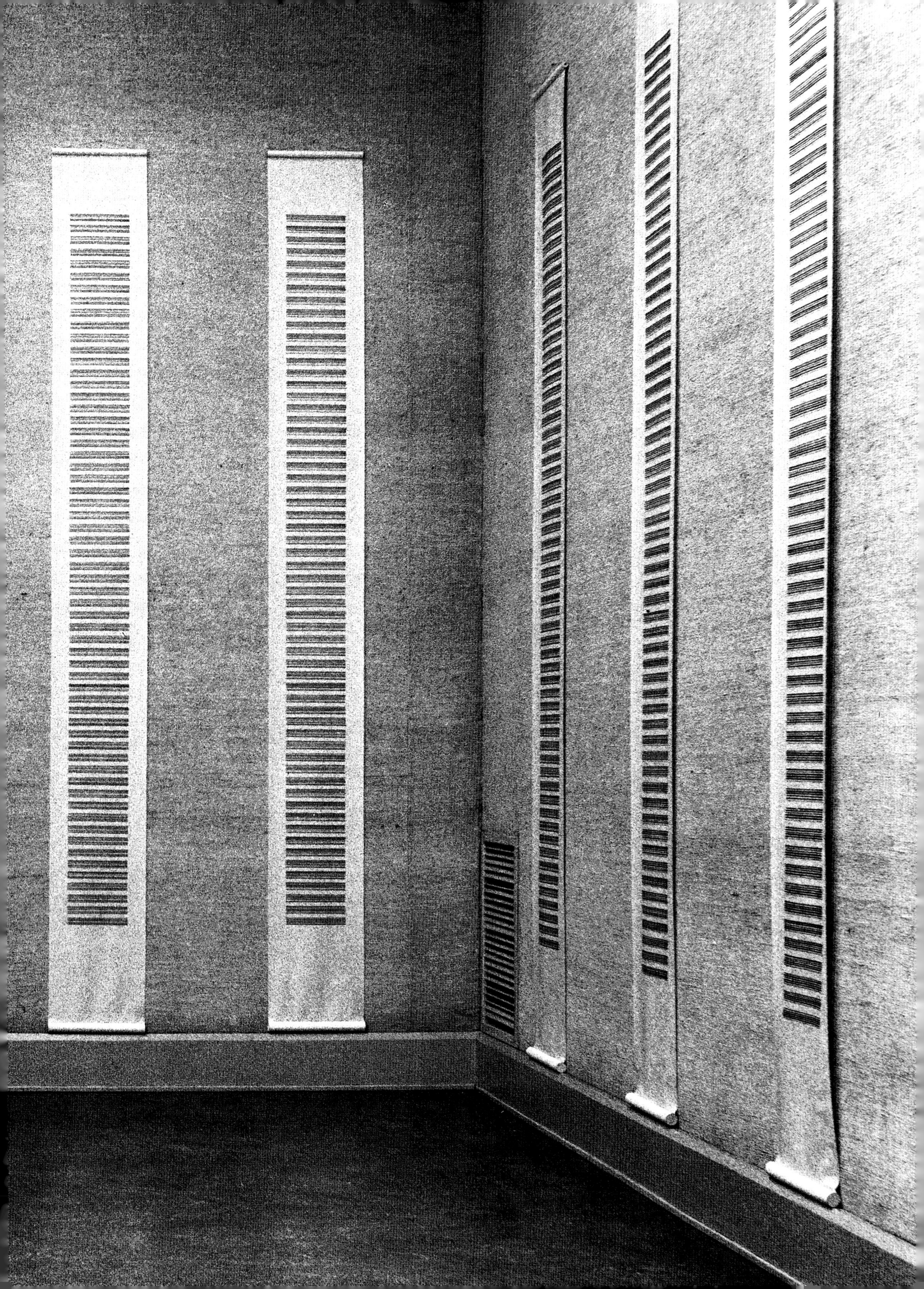

Variations—Coins
Arrangement in mathematical permutations
hypothetically changes the usual economic and social
symbolism of the coins, giving them an equal value.

Drawings for Coins *(details),*
1975
48 drawings on Japanese rice
paper
Each drawing 12⅛ × 9⁹⁄₁₆ inches
(30 × 23 cm)

Preceding pages and below:
Coins (details), 1975
*120 color photographs mounted
on board
Each photograph 3⅛ × 4½
inches (8 × 11.5 cm)*

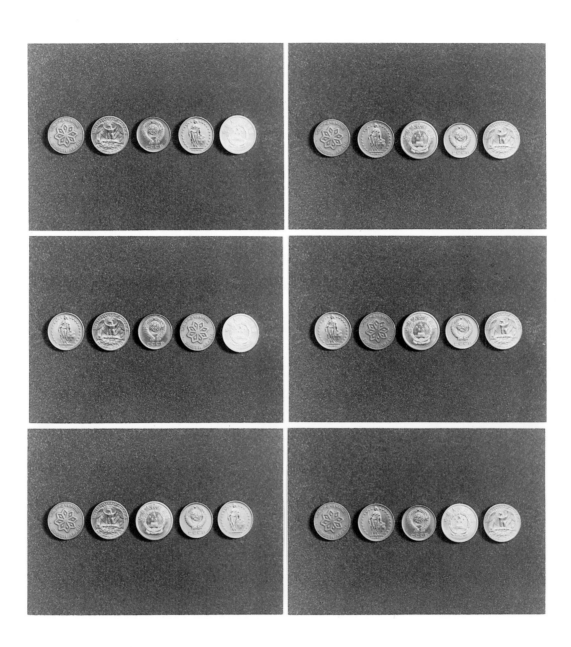

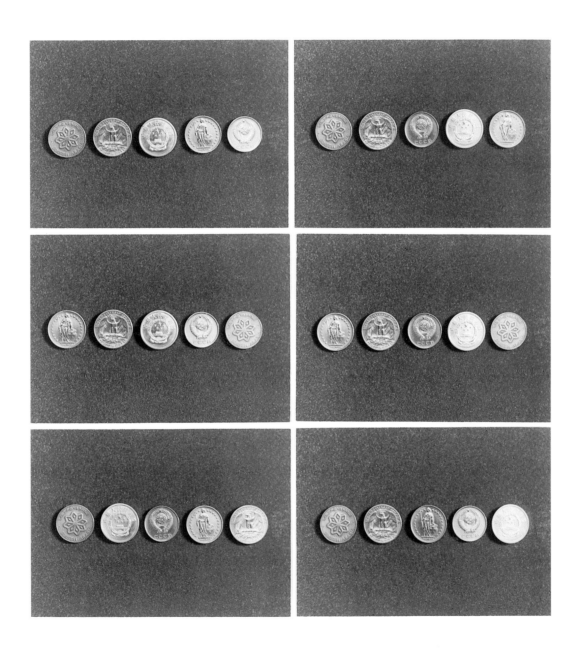

Variations—Hypothesis About Time

Three hundred and sixty photographs of a clock were taken at an interval of a second.

The work is based on a mathematical system of permutation applied to seconds: the unit of measure of the intervals of time.

The distinction that we perceive between the past, the present, and the future is related to the classic notion of time as a serial, homogeneous order. But time can be considered in relation to infinity in a different aspect, in which future, present, or past can succeed each other in another order.

The seconds of the clock go forward as well as backward in a passage of time in which future and past switch order and direction.

Hypothesis about Time *(detail)*,
1975
Panel two. Collection Leo
Castelli, New York

173

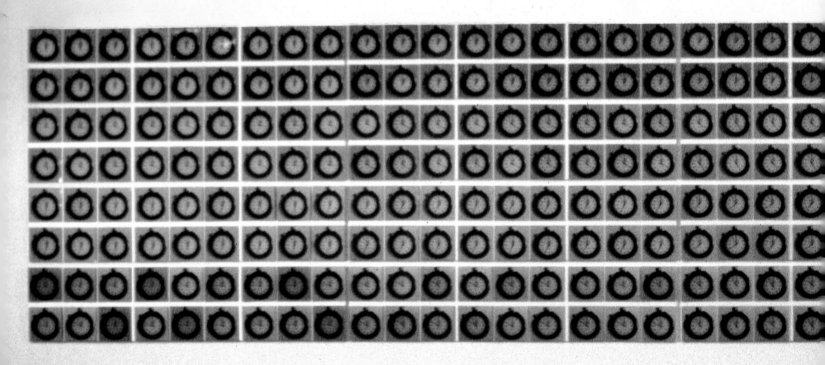

Hypothesis about Time, *1975*
Installation view at the Leo
Castelli Gallery, New York, 1976

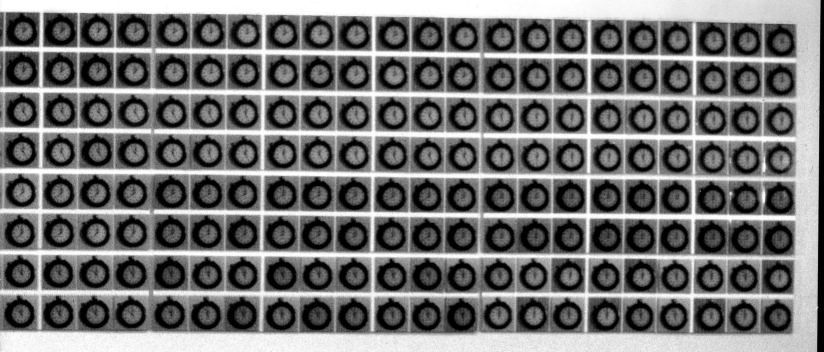

Variations—Hypothesis About Space

A hexagon that rotates on its side produces six hexagons. After six turns the same position would be repeated if the rotation were continued. My hypothesis is that each one of these hexagons, continuing the rotation in space, will produce a different hexagon, and continuing this movement the hexagons will progressively multiply. This is possible only if we consider that the rotation happens in a space whose dimension is also perceived relative to the dynamic of time (a fourth dimension). Only in this way can we understand that the hexagons are always different. Their progressive rotations could continue to infinity.

Right:
Hypothesis about Space *(detail),*
1975
266 color photographs mounted
on board
Each hexagon 4¾ × 5 inches
(12 × 12.5 cm)

The Imaginary Dimension
Rotated to Infinity Hypothesis:
Space-Time *(detail)*, 1975
Ink on paper
Seven parts, each 27½ × 19¾
inches (69.8 × 50.1 cm)
Collection Leo Castelli,
New York

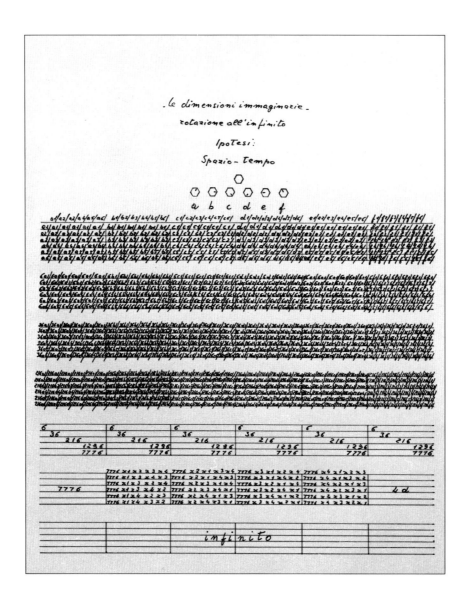

Below:
Space-Time Hexagonal Rotation,
1975
Ink on paper
9½ × 12 inches
(24.2 × 30.4 cm)

Following pages:
Hypothesis about Space *(detail),*
1975
Installation view at the Van
Abbemuseum, Eindhoven, 1976

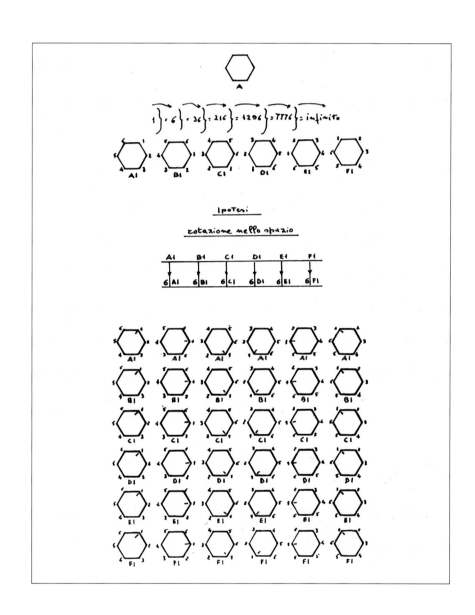

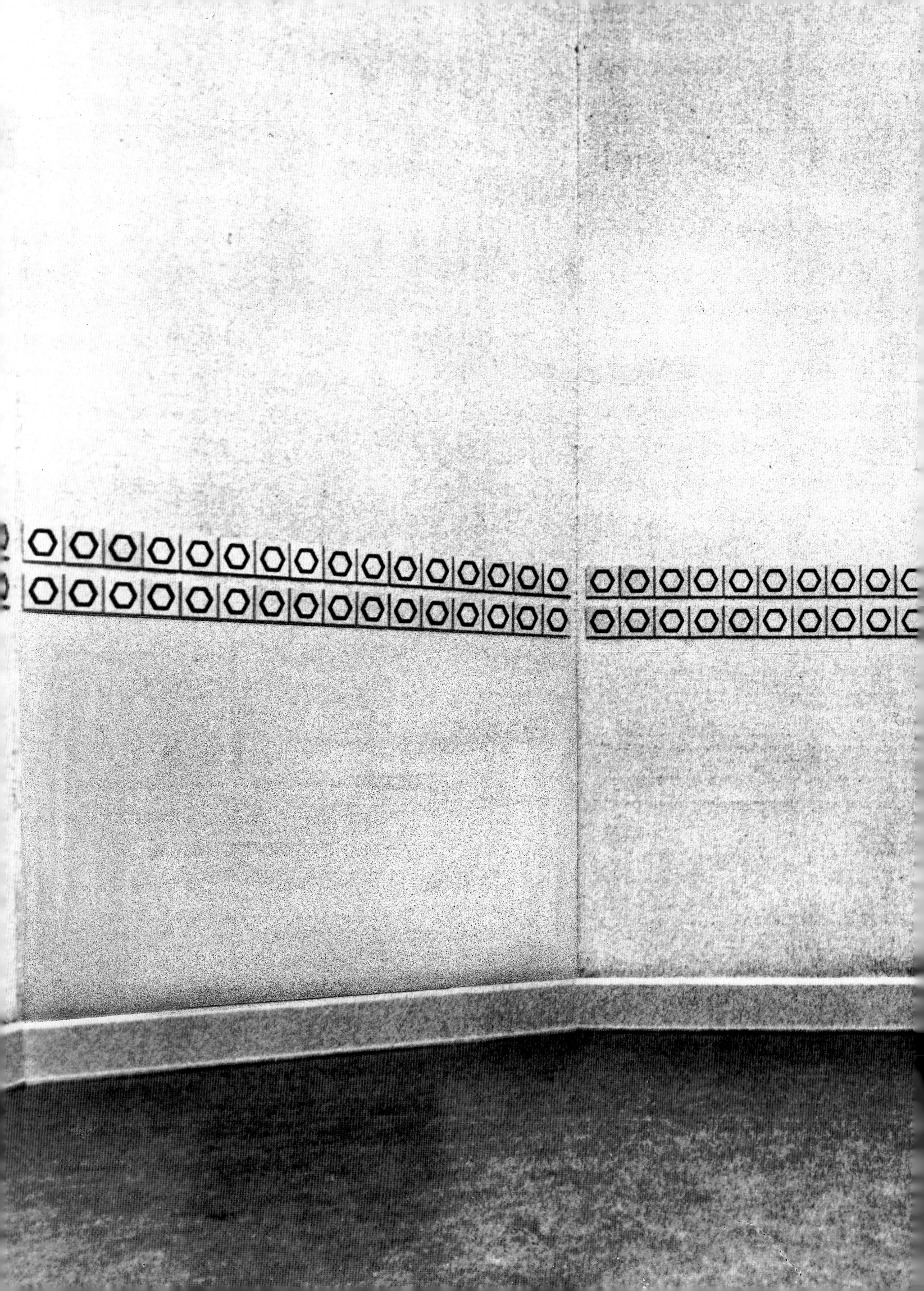

Variations—Similarities: Rondo

The rondo, both in its musical form and in the verse from which it originally derives, the rondel, repeats itself continuously in a circular rhythm, without altering its scheme. Thus it can be considered an unending melodic structure, just as the progressive rotation of hexagons can be considered an unending geometric structure: both can continue indefinitely.

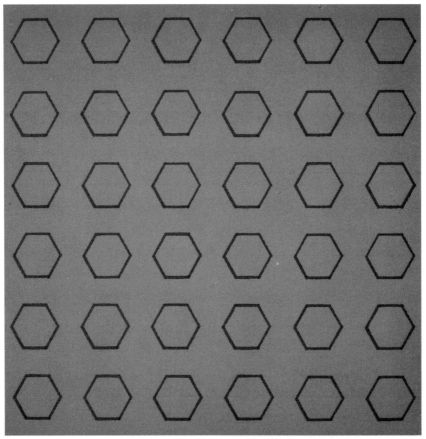

Above, right, and following pages:
Similarities: Rondo *(details),*
1976
216 color photographs repeating the image of 7,776 hexagons, and four introductory photographs, including one of the rondo from Bach's Sixth Violin Solo
Each hexagon photograph
5⅛ × 5⅛ inches (13 × 13 cm)

RONDO

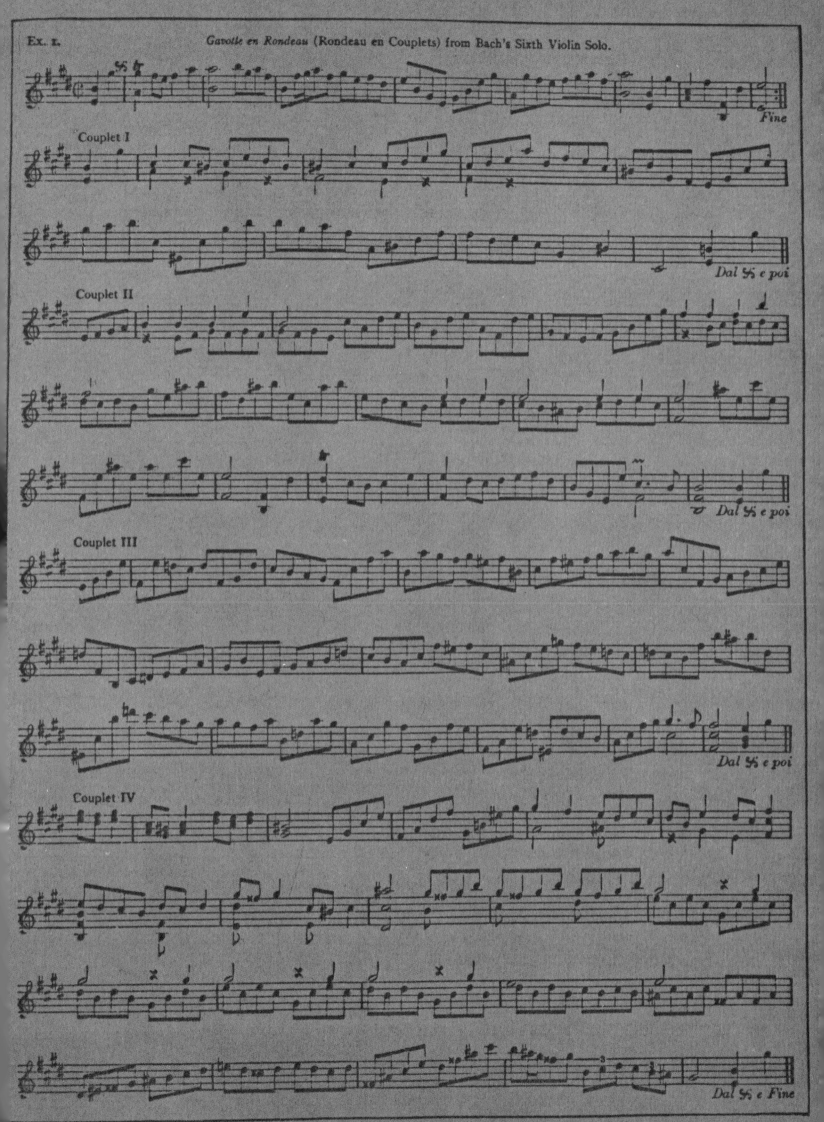

Ex. 1.

Gavotte en Rondeau (Rondeau en Couplets) from Bach's Sixth Violin Solo.

Fine

Couplet I

Dal 𝄋 e poi

Couplet II

Dal 𝄋 e poi

Couplet III

Dal 𝄋 e poi

Couplet IV

RONDO

Dal 𝄋 e Fine

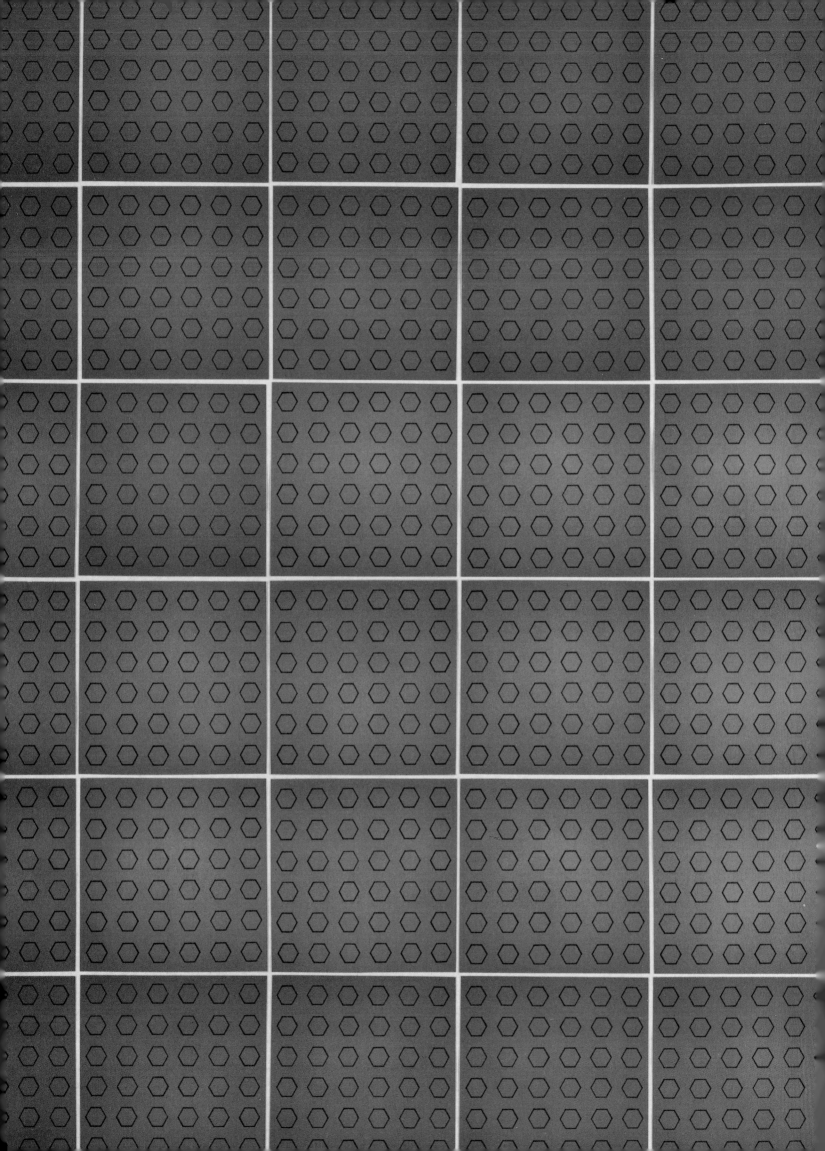

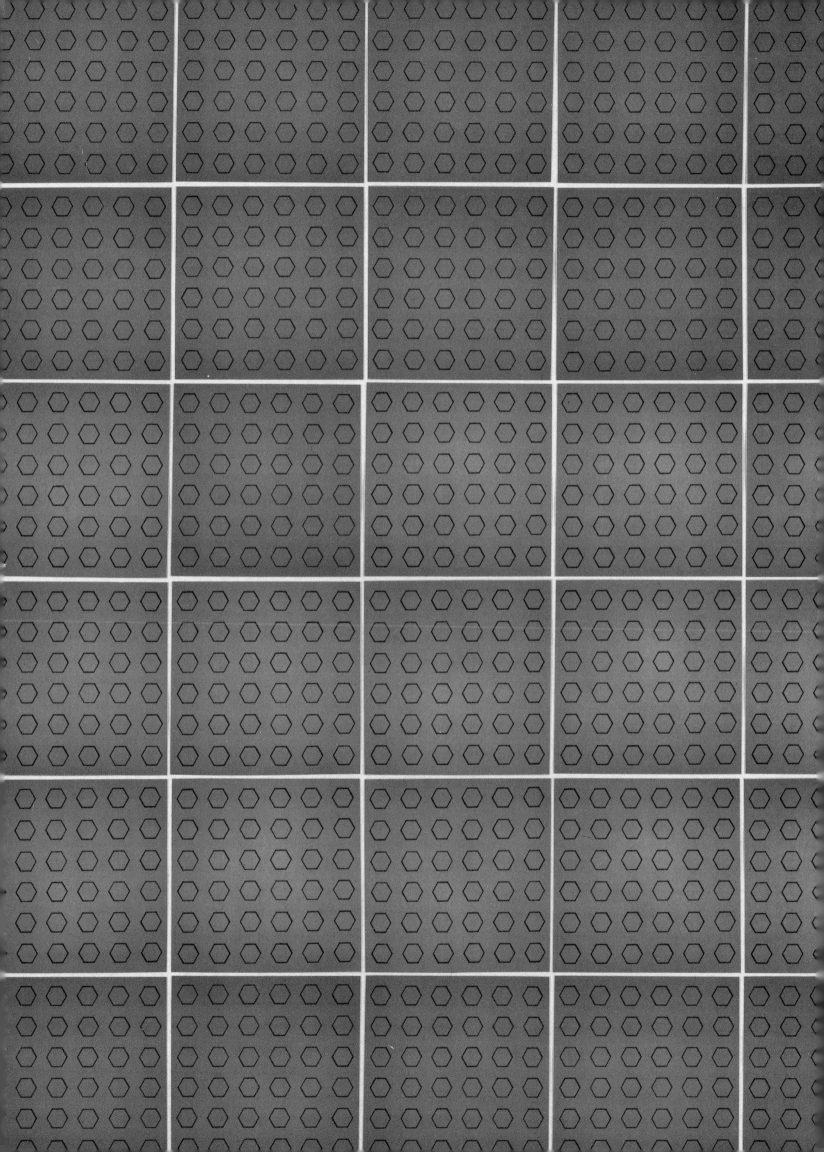

De More Geometrico—Endless Dialogue
This group is related to the notion that the continuity
of space, the duration of an event, and the time in
which it is perceived are all divisible ad infinitum,
and that a whole is divisible into smaller identical
parts, reflecting itself back in an infinitely divisible
reflective form.

In *Endless Dialogue* the surface of a chessboard is
divided into countless smaller squares. It is traversed
by a tortoise, who, on reaching the last square, finds
there another chessboard—itself also infinitely
divisible. The last term of this process is the infinite.

After the tortoise has crossed each board, only to
start again in the last square, the preceding
chessboard, including the tortoise in it, becomes part
of the new one.

$$10 + \frac{1}{10} + \frac{1}{10}^{2} + \frac{1}{10}^{3} + \frac{1}{10}^{4} + \frac{1}{10}^{5} + \frac{1}{10}^{6}$$

$$+ \frac{1}{10}^{7} + \frac{1}{10}^{8} + \frac{1}{10}^{9} + \frac{1}{10}^{10} + \frac{1}{10}^{11} + \frac{1}{10}^{12} + \frac{1}{10}^{13} + \frac{1}{10}^{14}$$

$$+ \frac{1}{10}^{15} + \frac{1}{10}^{16} + \frac{1}{10}^{17} + \frac{1}{10}^{18} + \frac{1}{10}^{19} + \frac{1}{10}^{20} + \frac{1}{10}^{21} + \frac{1}{10}^{22}$$

$$+ \frac{1}{10}^{23} + \frac{1}{10}^{24} + \frac{1}{10}^{25} + \frac{1}{10}^{26} + \frac{1}{10}^{27} + \frac{1}{10}^{28} + \frac{1}{10}^{29} + \frac{1}{10}^{30}$$

$$+ \frac{1}{10}^{31} + \frac{1}{10}^{32} + \frac{1}{10}^{33} + \frac{1}{10}^{34} + \frac{1}{10}^{35} + \frac{1}{10}^{36} + \frac{1}{10}^{37} + \frac{1}{10}^{38}$$

$$+ \frac{1}{10}^{39} + \frac{1}{10}^{40} + \frac{1}{10}^{41} + \frac{1}{10}^{42} + \frac{1}{10}^{43} + \frac{1}{10}^{44} + \frac{1}{10}^{45} + \frac{1}{10}^{46}$$

$$+ \frac{1}{10}^{47} + \frac{1}{10}^{48} + \frac{1}{10}^{49} + \frac{1}{10}^{50} + \frac{1}{10}^{51} + \frac{1}{10}^{52} + \frac{1}{10}^{53} + \frac{1}{10}^{54}$$

$$+ \frac{1}{10}^{55} + \frac{1}{10}^{56} + \frac{1}{10}^{57} + \frac{1}{10}^{58} + \frac{1}{10}^{59} + \frac{1}{10}^{... } + \frac{1}{10}^{infinito}$$

infinito

Endless Dialogue *(detail), 1977*

Endless Dialogue *(detail), 1977*

Endless Dialogue *(detail)*, 1977

Endless Dialogue *(detail), 1977*

Endless Dialogue *(detail), 1977*

Endless Dialogue *(detail), 1977*

Following pages:
Endless Dialogue, *1977*
Installation view at the Galerie
Konrad Fischer, Düsseldorf,
1978

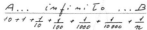

$$A \dots \text{infinito} \dots B$$
$$10 + 1 + \frac{1}{10} + \frac{1}{100} + \frac{1}{1000} + \frac{1}{10\,000} + \frac{1}{n}$$

Above:
Endless Dialogue *(detail), 1978*

Right:
Endless Dialogue, *1978*
Nine drawings in pen and ink
Each drawing 17¾ × 17¾
inches (45 × 45 cm)
Collection The Museum of
Modern Art, New York.
Gift of Leo Castelli

197

De More Geometrico—Minimum Discernible

This work is about visual perception, and the idea
that the duration of an event and the time in which we
perceive it are divisible into progressively shorter
periods of time, arriving finally at a moment so short
that it allows no further division while remaining
visible: the minimum discernible. Fixed in a
photograph, the flight of two birds is used as an event
of a perceptible duration. It is subjected to a
continuous process of division, until it reaches the
minimum discernible. This is the last image of the
work: a point within which the image of the flight is
visible, but only using a lens. The image can still be
divided, but because of the precariousness of visual
data, it will diminish beyond our ability to perceive it.

Right:
Minimum Discernible *(detail)*,
1977
14 color photographs
Each photograph 9½ × 7 inches
(24 × 18 cm)
Collection Antonio De Sanctis,
Rome

Minimum Discernible *(details)*,
1977

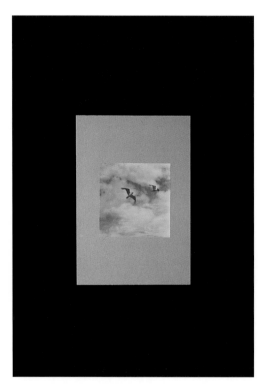
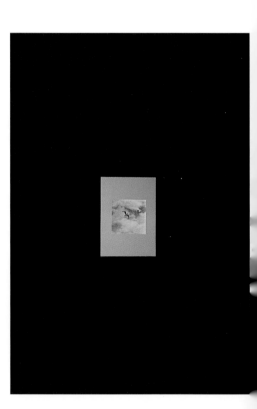

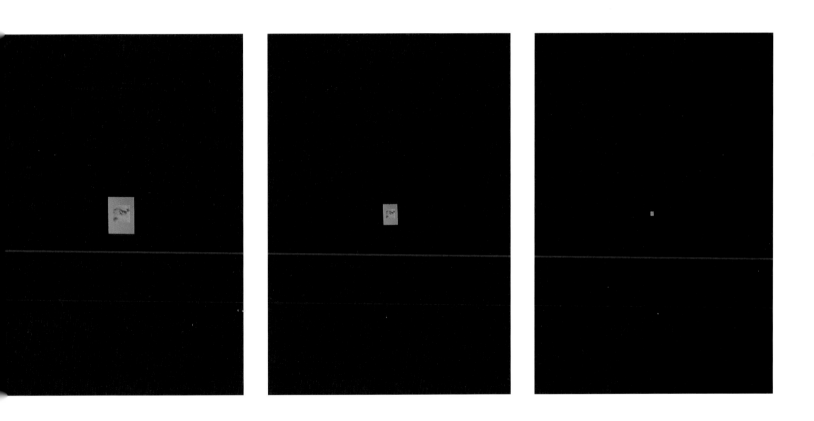

De More Geometrico—Reflectivity

An infinite whole can have parts that are identical to it; the wholeness is reflected in the part, though the part is smaller than the whole. By the same relation, the part is reflected in a smaller one, as in an endless specular series infinitely reflecting itself. The use of an image already in itself reflective (a figure in a landscape looks at its own simultaneous image, and finds itself reflected in it again . . .) describes the repetitive process that defines the infinite equivalence of reflectivity.

Reflectivity *(details), 1977*
15 panels: 7 color photographs
and 8 drawings in ink on paper
mounted on canvas
Each panel 28 × 20 inches
(71 × 51 cm)

De More Geometrico—Blue Triangle

A triangle, divisible into smaller and smaller spaces, is traversed by a bird that, before being able to cross it, encounters another space infinitely divisible, which is another triangle.

The bird wishes to cover the entire distance. However, at the point at which it thinks it may reach the end, it inevitably faces a final space that is also infinitely divisible, a new, and certainly final, triangle. . . .

The bird in this new triangle notes that the distance already covered—the preceding triangles (and the bird itself within them)—has become small and remote: a triangle, a triangle within a triangle. . . .

At this point the bird understands that the triangle, an apparently finite form, can be none other than the fragment of another identical but infinite form: an infinitely divisible reflexive form. Hence the bird begins its flight again in a space that, by now, it knows it can never traverse.

Blue Triangle *(detail), 1980*
Ink on cardboard, color
photographs, wood
121 pieces, each 9⅛ × 10½
inches (23 × 26 cm); overall
size 100 × 115 inches
(254 × 294 cm)
Collection Leo Castelli,
New York
One piece from the total of 121.

Triangle with Two Birds, *1980*
119 drawings in ink on paper,
2 color photographs, wood
121 pieces, each 9⅛ × 10½
inches (23 × 26 cm); overall
size 100 × 115 inches
(254 × 294 cm)

Blue Triangle, *1980*
Ink on cardboard, color
photographs, wood
121 pieces, each 9⅛ × 10½
inches (23 × 26 cm); overall
size 100 × 115 inches
(254 × 294 cm)
Collection Leo Castelli,
New York

Following pages:
Blue Triangle *(detail), 1980*

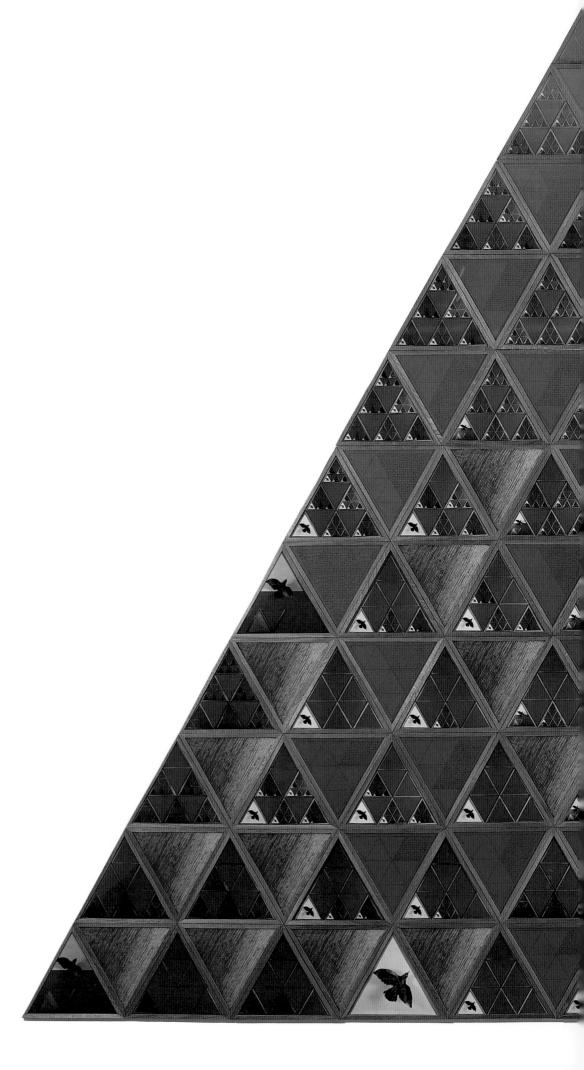

De More Geometrico—Scheherazade

The last of the trilogy that includes *Endless Dialogue*
(based on the square) and *Blue Triangle* (based on the
triangle), the *Scheherazade* works also follow the
division of a geometrical form—now the hexagon—
into countless smaller versions of itself. They
resemble the prismatic vision of a butterfly, closed off
in an infinitely divisible hexagonal space.

Right:
Scheherazade Part 1, *1982*
37 hexagons in color
photographs, wood, and collage
Each hexagon 8⅛ × 9⅜ inches
(21 × 24.5 cm); overall size
59 × 53½ inches (150 × 136 cm)

Below:
Scheherazade Part 2, *1982*
37 hexagons in tempera on
cardboard, wood, and collage
Each hexagon 8⅛ × 9⅜ inches
(21 × 24.5 cm); overall size
59 × 53½ inches (150 × 136 cm)

Right:
Scheherazade Part 3, *1982*
37 hexagons in color
photographs, wood, and collage
Each hexagon 8⅛ × 9⅜ inches
(21 × 24.5 cm); overall size
59 × 53½ inches (150 × 136 cm)

Following pages:
Scheherazade Part 3 *(detail),*
1982

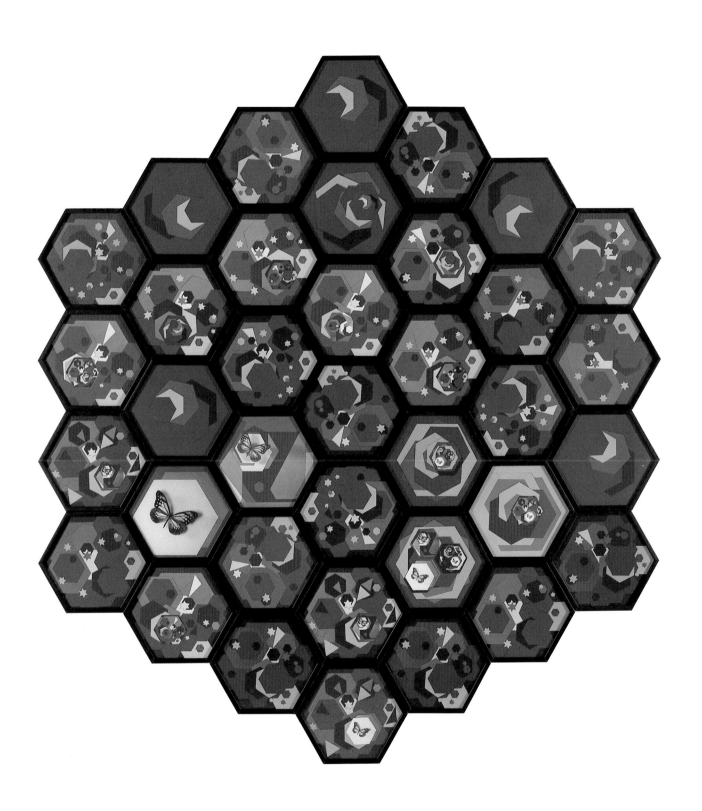

Sundials and Wall Sculptures

Sundials

All these sculptures are sundials. Some of them, realized in the open air, would measure the time like real sundials, by creating shadows to follow the changing of the sun's rays.

Sundial Reflections, *1985*
Wood, bronze, brass, marble
21⅝ × 13⅜ × 9¾ inches
(55 × 34 × 24 cm)
Collection Leo Castelli,
New York

Eclipse, *1985*
Wood, granite, marble
19½ × 17½ × 5⅝ inches
(49.5 × 44.5 × 14.5 cm)
Collection Leo Castelli,
New York

Moondial, *1985*
Wood, granite, marble
14⅜ × 13 × 6½ inches
(36.5 × 33 × 16.5 cm)
Collection Leo Castelli,
New York

Time Geometry, *1985*
Wood, brass, marble
16½ × 14 × 4½ inches
(42 × 36 × 11 cm)
Collection Leo Castelli,
New York

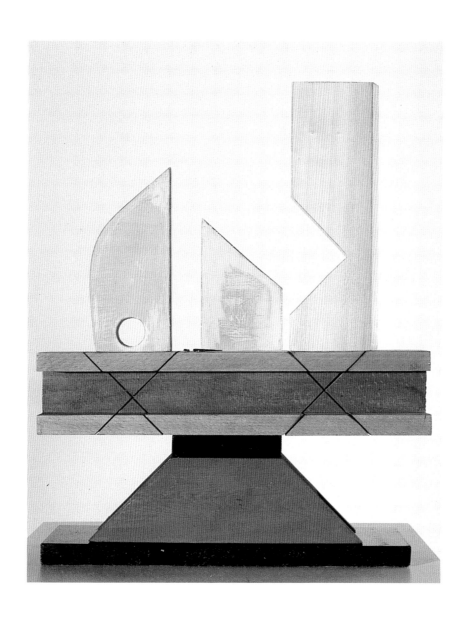

Installation view of wall sculptures at the Leo Castelli Greene Street Gallery, New York, 1986

Wall Sculptures

If we think of everything as existing in the arc of an infinite time, and in an infinite space, then everything at a certain point will be repeated. These next pieces are related to this concept of time, which implies the same notions that were contained in my preceding ones—notions of reflectivity, symmetry, similarity, and divisibility to infinity. These wall sculptures are three-dimensional paintings made on wood. They include smaller objects in cast bronze, brass, and other materials, and the wood surfaces are painted with wax and pigments. Some of the objects can be removed from the sculptures, or placed in other positions. Some of them are hidden—only on opening a small section can we see them. The various materials all have their own linguistic connotations: sometimes I painted with gold, which reflects light, increasing the sense of three-dimensionality, and elsewhere mosaic appears, or marble. Together, the works represent different art-historical meanings and periods, taken out of their usual contexts to be focused in a new one.

In *Classical Symmetry*, I wanted to represent the Renaissance perspective, based on a single point of view, and the mathematical law of symmetry—both of them opposed to the fourth-dimensional perspectives I had been exploring earlier, which deal with stratified levels of time and with variable viewpoints in space. The piece repeats two similar bunches of grapes, and the etched tablet between them shows how two similar figures are symmetrical when three points on each form's surface can be connected by three hypothetical lines that pass through the same center.

Right:
Classical Symmetry, *1985*
Wood, wax, bronze, granite, plaster
85⅞ × 57⅞ × 8⅝ inches
(218 × 147 × 22 cm)
Collection Mr. and Mrs. Thomas E. Worrell, Jr., Charlottesville, Virginia

Wall Sculptures—Apollinaire's Secret

Apollinaire's Secret includes a working hourglass that viewers can turn to measure the time. Near it is a clockface without hands—a "timeless" clock. On a plaster shelf are two books: a little volume of Dante, a 19th-century edition of *La Vita Nuova*, is to be taken out and read, while an identical book, cast in bronze, remains on the shelf: similarity and repetition, the one and its double. The bronze egg in the oval refers to Piero della Francesca's Urbino fresco.

Right:
Apollinaire's Secret, *1985*
Wood, wax, aluminum, bronze,
brass, marble, granite, plaster
85⅞ × 60½ × 6¾ inches
(218 × 153 × 17 cm)
Collection Frederick R.
Weisman, Los Angeles

Following pages:
Apollinaire's Secret *(detail), 1985*

Wall Sculptures—Gravity

A bronze apple is fixed in mid fall, as if defying gravity, and a round bronze basket is suspended sideways, as if gravity had emptied it. The references are to the laws of Isaac Newton.

Right:
Gravity, *1985*
Wood, wax, bronze
85⅞ × 56⅞ × 5⅞ inches
(218 × 144.5 × 15 cm)
Collection Leo Castelli,
New York

Following pages:
Gravity *(detail), 1985*

Wall Sculptures—Diary

Diary is an autobiographical work: cast in bronze are images of earlier pieces—clocks, a chessboard with a tortoise in a small box, hexagons, triangles. This is a personal labyrinth and a labyrinth of objects, a kind of diary of many different interests with a plurality of meanings.

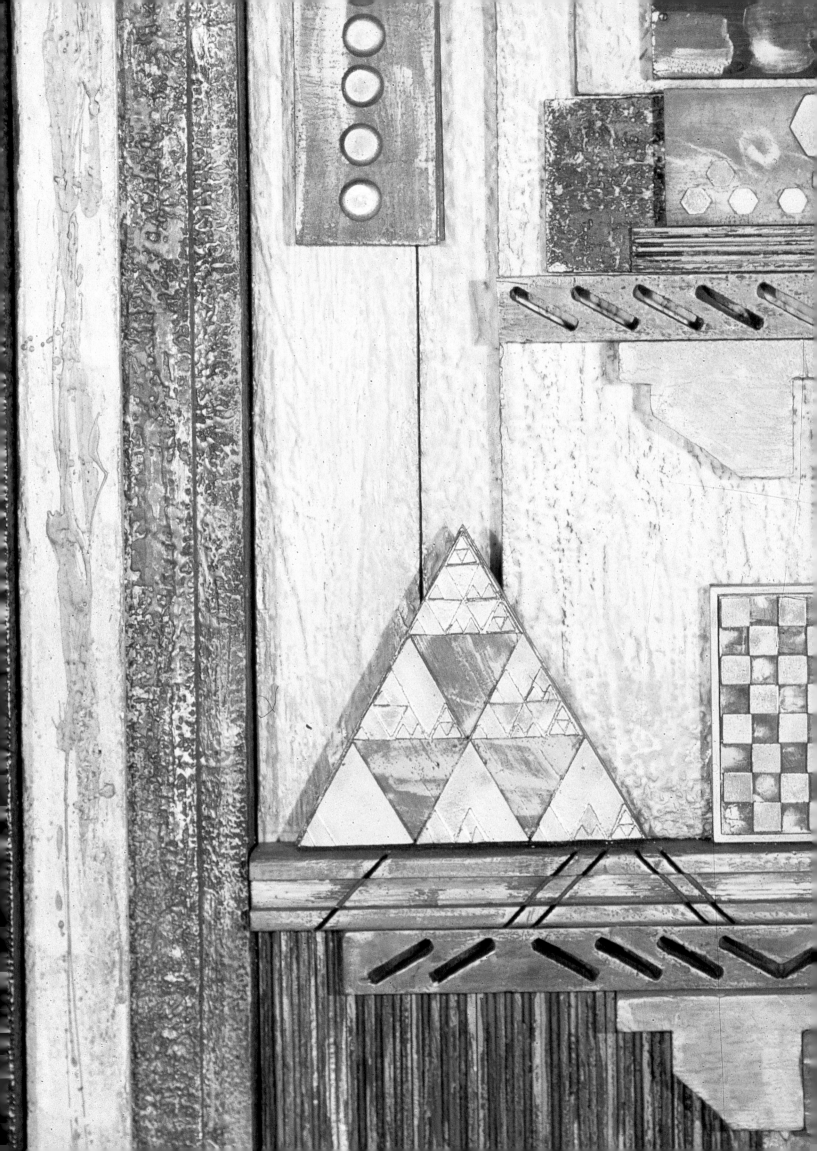

Wall Sculptures—Parmenides's Moon

This piece is inspired by the Greek philosopher Parmenides's concept of the one and the many, the unit and the multiplicity.

Right:
Parmenides's Moon, *1985*
Wood, canvas, wax, bronze,
brass, marble, mosaic
85⅞ × 57⅝ × 4¾ inches
(218 × 146.5 × 12 cm)
Collection Mr. and Mrs.
Thomas E. Worrell, Jr.,
Hillsboro, Florida

Following pages:
Parmenides's Moon *(detail), 1985*

Wall Sculptures—Borromini's Violin

Borromini's Violin is about reflectivity: the bronze violin is reflected in a small identical copy hidden in an oval box in the center, and etched in the bronze tablet on the wooden shelf is the repetitive melodic structure of the Bach Sixth Violin Solo, a rondo—a reflective musical image.

Right:
Borromini's Violin, *1985*
Wood, canvas, wax, bronze, marble
85⅞ × 60¼ × 5¾ inches
(218 × 153 × 14.5 cm)
Collection Mr. and Mrs. Thomas E. Worrell, Jr., Charlottesville, Virginia

Following pages:
Borromini's Violin *(detail), 1985*

Wall Sculptures—Mechanics

Mechanics, like *Gravity*, refers to the laws of Isaac
Newton—this time to the laws of mechanics. In
Newtonian vision, the whole universe can be seen as a
great machine. So here, cast in bronze, are objects
and symbols of the mechanical world view.

Right:
Mechanics, *1985*
Wood, canvas, wax, aluminum,
bronze, copper wire, granite,
plaster
85⅞ × 57⅞ × 6½ inches
(218 × 147 × 16.5 cm)
Collection Leo Castelli,
New York

Following pages:
Mechanics *(detail), 1985*

Wall Sculptures—Still Life

The canvas on the easel in *Still Life* holds not a painted image but a sculptural one. On a shelf on the easel are the tools usually used for modeling clay. This ambiguity of appearance introduces a shift of meaning: a sense of positive and negative. Three bronze squares engraved with fractional numbers suggest a unit divided in a series of divisions that progresses to infinity.

Right:
Still Life, *1985*
Wood, canvas, wax, bronze, marble
85⅞ × 56⅞ × 7⅛ inches
(218 × 144.5 × 18 cm)
Collection Eugenio Buontempo, Rome

Following pages:
Still Life *(detail), 1985*

Wall Sculptures—Hillsboro Venus

Hidden in small compartments, and visible by opening the boxes' lids, are a number of cast-bronze objects related to the law of dynamics—a helicopter, a Lear jet, a Harley Davidson, and other symbols of movement and speed. The work also contains different instruments of navigation, and within its portholelike ring, one sees the shell from Botticelli's *Birth of Venus*.

Exhibition History, Bibliography
and Biographical Images from
1965 to 1990

UNA DONNA
FRA I TUAREG

Laura
Quilici

One-Person Exhibitions	1965

One-Person Exhibitions

1965
Galleria dell'Ariete, Milan (January).

1968
Galerie E. M. Thelen, Essen (January).

1969
Galleria Marlborough, Rome, "*Un Area di Nebbia*" (May 21).

1970
Galleria del Naviglio, Milan (February 18).
Galeria E. M. Thelen, Cologne (April–May).

1973
Leo Castelli, New York, "Pebbles" (May 19–June 6).

1975
Leo Castelli, New York, "Stripes" (May 10–24).
Castelli Graphics, New York, "Stripes" (May 24–June 7).
Saman Gallery, Genoa (October).

1976
Françoise Lambert, Milan (January).
Leo Castelli, New York, "Hypothesis about Time"
(April 24–May 15).
Van Abbemuseum, Eindhoven (September 10–October 10).

1977
Galleria Marilena Bonomo, Bari (January).

1978
Saman Gallery, Genoa (May).
Galerie Konrad Fischer, Düsseldorf
(September 16–October 10).
Leo Castelli, New York (October 28–November 18).

1979
Ugo Ferranti, Rome (January).

1980
Françoise Lambert, Milan (April 2–20).

1981
Leo Castelli, New York (March 7–28).
Ugo Ferranti, Rome (October).

1986
Leo Castelli Greene Street Gallery, New York (February 8–
March 1).

Group Exhibitions

1965
Quadriennale, Rome

1966
XXXIII Biennale, Venice (June 18–October 16).
"Italy New Tendencies," Galleria Bonino, New York.
"*Rassegna Arti Figurative*," Amalfi.

1967
"*Mostra Nazionale Premio Trento*"
(October 11–November 10).
"*Museo Sperimentale d'Arte Contemporanea*," Galleria Civica
d'Arte Moderna, Turin (April).

1968
"Young Italians," Institute of Contemporary Art, Boston
(January 23–March 23).
The exhibition traveled to The Jewish Museum,
New York (May 20–September 2).
"*Teatro delle Mostre*," Galleria La Tartaruga, Rome.
Galerie E. M. Thelen, Kassel.
"*Prospect 68*," Kunsthalle Düsseldorf.

1969
"*I Materiali*," Qui Arte Contemporanea, Rome.
"*Nuovi Materiali, Nuove Tecniche*," Caorle, Venice.
"*Plane und Projekte als Kunst*," Kunsthalle Bern.
"Plans and Projects as Art," Actionsraum 1, Munich.
Galleria Diagramma, Milan.

268

1970
"*Grafica italiana d'oggi*," Palazzo Reale, Naples.
"*Kunst nach Planen*," Kunsthaus Hamburg.
"*Arte e critica 70*," Modena.

1971
"Earth Air Fire Water: Elements of Art,"
Museum of Fine Arts, Boston.

1972
"*Mappa 72*," Incontri Internazionali d'Arte, Rome.

1973
X Quadriennale, Rome.
"Italy Two: Art around 70," Philadelphia Civic Center
"*Contemporanea*," Villa Borghese, Rome
(November 1973–February 1974).

1974
"*De Matematica*," Galleria l'Obelisco, Rome.
"*Grafica Internazionale*," Museo d'Arte Moderna, Turin.

1977
"Time," Philadelphia College of Art (April 15–May 21).

1978
"*Le figure del tempo*," Galleria de Foscherari, Bologna.
"Numerals 1924–1977," Leo Castelli Gallery, New York
(January 7–28). The exhibition traveled to the Yale University
Art Gallery, New Haven, Connecticut (February 14–March
26); the Dartmouth College Museum and Galleries, Hopkins
Center, Hanover, New Hampshire (April 21–May 21); the
University Art Gallery, University of North Dakota, Grand
Forks (August 29–September 26); the Minneapolis College of
Art & Design, Minnesota (October 4–November 1); the Fine
Arts Gallery, University of California, Irvine (November 10–
December 10); the Art Museum of South Texas, Corpus
Christi (January 5, 1979–February 4, 1979); the Center for the
Visual Arts Gallery, Illinois State University, Normal
(February 17–March 16, 1979); the Center for the Arts,
Muhlenberg College, Allentown, Pennsylvania (March 30–
April 28, 1979); and the New Gallery of Contemporary Art,
Cleveland, Ohio (May 15–June 15, 1979).

1979
"Intricate Structure/Repeated Image, Part I," Tyler School of
Art, Temple University, Philadelphia, Pennsylvania
(January 19–February 10).

1980
"Intricate Structure/Repeated Image, Part II," Tyler School of
Art, Temple University, Philadelphia, Pennsylvania
(January 21–February 10).
"*Cronografie: Il tempo e la memoria*," a special project of the
Venice Biennale.

1981
"*Linea della ricerca artistica in Italia 1960–1980*," Palazzo
delle Esposizioni, Rome (February 14–April 15).
"*Erweiterte Fotografie*," Biennale V, Vienna.

1982
"Group Show," Saman Gallery, Genoa (February–March).
"Castelli and His Artists—Twenty-Five Years," organized by
the Aspen Center for the Visual Arts, Colorado. The
exhibition traveled to the La Jolla Museum of Contemporary
Art, California (April 23–June 6); the Aspen Center for the
Visual Arts (June 17–August 7); the Leo Castelli Gallery, New
York (September 11–October 9); the Portland Center for the
Visual Arts, Oregon (October 22–December 3); and the
Laguna Gloria Art Museum, Austin, Texas
(December 17–February 13, 1983).

1983
"Drawings—Photographs," Leo Castelli Gallery, New York
(June 11 through summer).

1985
"*Il museo sperimentale di Torino: Arte italiana negli anni sessanta nelle collezioni della Galleria Civica d'Arte Moderna,*" Castello di Rivoli, Turin (December 1985–February 1986).

1986
Quadriennale, Rome.
XLII Biennale, Venice (June–October).
"*Surrealismo,*" Barbara Braathen Gallery, New York.

1987
Thirtieth Anniversary Show, "The First Fifteen Years: Part 2," Leo Castelli Greene Street Gallery, New York (March 14–April 4).
"*Leo Castelli y sus artistas,*" Centro Cultural Arte Contemporaneo, Mexico City (June–October).
"Leo Castelli: A Tribute Exhibition," Butler Institute of American Art, Youngstown, Ohio (June 28–September 27).
"Three Decades of Exploration: Homage to Leo Castelli," Fort Lauderdale Museum, Florida (October 1987–January 1988).

1988
"In Memory of Toini Castelli," The Mayor Gallery, London (May 19–June 23).

1990
"The Artists of Leo Castelli," Nichido Gallery, Tokyo (February 9–19).

Video and Audiotapes, Films	*Wind Speed*, 1968, black and white film in 16 mm, 15 minutes, with sound.
	The Measuring of Time, 1969, black and white film in 16 mm.
	Whirlpool, 1971, color film in 16 mm.
	Sounds, 1971, two audio cassette tapes, 15 minutes each side.
	From One to Four Pebbles, 1972, color videotape and color film in 16 mm.
Books and texts by Laura Grisi	*Pasos por Buenos Aires*, Buenos Aires: Capricornio Editora, 1963.
	I Denti del Tigre, Milan: Lerici Editore, 1965.
	"*L'aria è la certezza visiva di uno spazio,*" in *Qui—Arte Contemporanea* 6, Rome, September 1969.
	Distillations: 3 Months of Looking, Macerata: Edizione Artestudio, 1970. Signed edition of 300 copies.
	Distillations: Choice and Choosing 16 from 5000, Macerata: Edizione Artestudio, 1970. Signed edition of 300 copies.
	In *Saman*, Genoa: untitled essay in December 1975–January 1976; untitled essay in October–November 1976; "*Riflessivita,*" March–April 1978; "*Dialogo senza fine,*" October–November 1978; untitled essay, April–May 1980.
	Endless Dialogue, Milan: Samanedizione e Vanni Scheiwiller, 1978.
	Statement in Arturo Schwarz et al., *Arte e alchimia*, Venice: La Biennale, and Milan: Electa, 1986.
Catalogues for one-person exhibitions	Renato Barilli, *Laura Grisi*, Milan: Galleria dell'Ariete, 1965.
	Udo Kultermann, *Laura Grisi*, Essen: Galerie E. M. Thelen, 1968.
	Giulio Carlo Argan, *Laura Grisi*, Cologne: Galerie E. M. Thelen, 1970.
	Laura Grisi, Milan: Galleria del Naviglio, 1970.
	Laura Grisi, Eindhoven: Van Abbemuseum, 1976.

Catalogues for group exhibitions

Quadriennale, Rome, 1965.

Nello Ponente, XXXIII Biennale, Venice, 1966.

Italy New Tendencies, New York: Galleria Bonino, 1966.

Rassegna Arti Figurative, Amalfi, 1966.

Maurizio Fagiolo dell'Arco, *Mostra Nazionale Premio Trento*, 1967.

Museo Sperimentale d'Arte Contemporanea, Turin, Galleria Civica d'Arte Moderna, Edizioni del Museo, 1967.

Alan Solomon, *Young Italians*, Boston: Institute of Contemporary Art, and New York: The Jewish Museum, 1968.

Prospect 68, Düsseldorf: Kunsthalle, 1968.

Nuovi Materiali, Nuove Tecniche, Caorle, Venice, 1969.

Nello Ponente, *Arte e critica 70*, Modena, 1970.

Earth Air Fire Water: Elements of Art, Boston: Museum of Fine Arts, 1971.

Quadriennale, Rome, 1973.

Italy Two: Art around '70, Philadelphia: Civic Center, 1973.

Contemporanea, Florence: Centro Di, 1973.

Leo Castelli Twenty Years, New York, 1977.

Le figure del tempo, Bologna: Galleria de'Foscherari, 1978.

Rainer Crone, *Numerals 1924–1977*, New York: Leo Castelli Gallery, 1978.

Lucy R. Lippard, *Intricate Structure/Repeated Image*, Philadelphia: Tyler School of Art, Temple University, 1979–80.

Cronografie: Il tempo e la memoria, Venice Biennale, 1980.

Linea della ricerca artistica in Italia 1960–1980, Rome: De Luca Editore, 1981.

Erweiterte Fotografie, Biennale V, Vienna, 1981.

Germano Celant, *Identité italienne—L'Art en Italie depuis 1959*, Paris: Centre Georges Pompidou, 1981.

Castelli and His Artists—Twenty-Five Years, Aspen, Colorado: Aspen Center for the Visual Arts, 1982.

Il museo sperimentale di Torino, Turin: Castello Di Rivoli, 1985.

Quadriennale, Rome, 1986.

Arturo Schwarz et al., *Arte e alchimia*, Venice: La Biennale, and Milan: Electa, 1986.

Leo Castelli y sus artistas, Mexico City: Centro Cultural Arte Contemporaneo, 1987.

Three Decades of Exploration: Homage to Leo Castelli, Fort Lauderdale: Fort Lauderdale Museum, Florida, 1987.

In Memory of Toini Castelli, London: The Mayor Gallery, 1988.

The Artists of Leo Castelli, Tokyo: Nichido Gallery, 1990.

Newspapers and Magazines

Gillo Dorfles, *Art International*, Lugano, March 1965.

Maurizio Fagiolo dell'Arco, *Avanti*, Rome, November 1965, June 1966.

F. Di Castro, *Le Arti*, Rome, June 1966.

Art International X no. 6, Lugano, 1966.

Marco Valsecchi, *Il Giorno*, Milan, June 1966.

Alain Jouffroy, *L'Oeil*, no. 139–140, Lausanne.

Pierre Restany, *Domus* no. 441, August 1966.

271

Giuseppe Gatt, *"Pop e Op verso l'integrazione?," Marcatre*, Lerici editore, Rome.

Cesare Vivaldi, *Qui—Arte Contemporanea* no. 2, Rome.

Nello Ponente, *Qui—Arte Contemporanea* no. 2, Rome.

Giovanni Carandente, *Prospettive di cultura* no. 4, 1966.

The New York Times, 26 October 1966.

Time, 4 November 1966.

Horst Laube, *Neue Ruhr Zeitung*, 13 January 1968.

Studio International, London, January 1968.

Heiner Stachelhaus, *Essener Tageblatt*, Essen, 13 January 1968.

"Mit neonlicht und plexiglas," Waz, 18 January 1968.

Patriot Ledger, Quincy, Mass., 2 February 1968.

Caron Le Brun, *Sunday Herald Traveler*, Boston, 4 February 1968.

Sunday Advertiser, Boston, January 1968.

David Shirey, "Young Italians," *Arts*, New York, June 1968.

Achille Bonito Oliva, *Sipario*, Milan, August 1968.

Domus no. 469, Milan, December 1968.

Cesare Vivaldi, *Collage 8*, Palermo, December 1968.

Qui—Arte Contemporanea no. 5, Rome, March 1969.

Das Kunstwerk, April–May 1969.

Vittorio Rubiu, *Corriere della Sera*, Milan, 15 June 1969.

Panorama, Milan, 3 July 1969.

Tommaso Trini, *Domus*, Milan, November 1969.

Tommaso Trini, *Domus* no. 484, Milan, March 1970.

Bolaffi Arte no. 4, 1970.

Art International XIV no. 8, Lugano, October 1970.

George Jappe, *Frankfurter Allgemeine Zeitung*, Frankfurt, 6 October 1971.

Kenneth Baker, "Boston," exhibition review, *Artforum* IX no. 7, New York, March 1971.

Robert Taylor, "A Bold Step Forward," exhibition review, *The Art Gallery Magazine* XIV no. 5, February 1971, pp. 72–74.

Alicia Faxon, "Earth Air Fire Water: Art's Nature, Nature's Art," *Boston After Dark*, Boston, 9 February 1971, p. 12.

Boston Arts, exhibition review, Boston, January–February 1971, p. 14.

Diane Loercher, "Elements of Art," exhibition review, *Christian Science Monitor*, Boston, 11 February 1971, p. 9.

Germano Beringheli, *"Le permutazioni di Laura Grisi," Il Lavoro*, Genoa, 23 December 1975.

"Ipotesi sul tempo," Domus no. 556, Milan, March 1976, p. 51.

"Laura Grisi," *Data 22*, Milan, July–September 1976, pp. 69–71.

"Laura Grisi," *Flash Art* 62–63, Milan, March 1976, pp. 32–34.

Art-Rite no. 14, New York, 1976–77, pp. 15–18.

"Laura Grisi," *Info-Artitudes* no. 4, January 1976.

Henry Martin, exhibition review, *Art International* 20, Lugano, March–April 1976, pp. 62–64.

Art Press 22, January–February 1976.

Tommaso Trini, *Corriere della Sera*, Milan, 25 January 1976.

Nello Ponente, "Laura Grisi," *Paese Sera*, Rome, 2 October 1976.

Vanni Scheiwiller, *L'Europeo*, Milan, 18 February 1977.

Viana Conti, *"Una storia del relativo: Laura Grisi," Corriere Mercantile*, Genoa, 19 May 1978.

Germano Celant, *La Repubblica*, Rome, 3 September 1978.

Robbie Erlich, "Laura Grisi," exhibition review, *Arts*, New York, December 1978.

"Cramer Puts Together Art and Music in Unusual Show," *Temple Times* 9 no. 8, 18 January 1979.

Achille Bonito Oliva, "Laura Grisi," *Corriere della Sera*, Milan, 8 February 1979.

Roberto G. Lambarelli, "Laura Grisi," exhibition review, *Flash Art*, international edition, Milan, March–April, 1979.

Flaminio Gualdoni, *"L'infinito è un triangolo," Il Giorno*, Milan, 23 April 1980.

Arturo C. Quintavalle, *"Cronografie*—Memory and Time," *Domus* no. 614, Milan, February 1981.

Filiberto Menna, *"Combinazioni d'artista—La pittura di Laura Grisi," Paese Sera*, Rome, 15 November 1981.

"Laura Grisi," *La Repubblica*, Rome, 23 October 1981.

Arte Bolaffi no. 128, March 1983.

Flash Art no. 134, Italian edition, Milan, 1986.

Frederick Ted Castle, "Occurrences/New York," *Art Monthly* 95, April 1986.

Gerrit Henry, "Laura Grisi at Castelli Greene St.," exhibition review, *Art in America*, New York, September 1986.

Books

Maurizio Calvesi, *Teatro delle Mostre*, Rome: Lerici Editore, 1969.

Udo Kultermann, *Neue Formen des Bildes*, Tubingen: Verlag Ernst Wasmuth, 1969.

Udo Kultermann, *Nuove forme della pittura*, Milan: Feltrinelli, 1969.

Alberto Boatto, *"Poetiche europee dell'oggettualitá," L'Arte Moderna*, vol. XIII, Milan: Fabbri Editori, 1969.

Soho: Downtown Manhattan, Akademie der Kunst, Berliner Festwochen, 1976.

Germano Celant, *Precronistoria 1966–69*, Florence: Centro Di, 1976.

Achille Bonito Oliva, *Autocritico Automobile—Attraverso le avanguardie*, Milan: Il Formichiere, 1977.

Germano Celant, *Off Media, Nuove techniche artistiche: Video disco libro*, Bari: Edizioni Dedalo, 1977.

Art Actuel, Geneva: Skira, 1977.

Photographs by:

Claudio Abate, Rome
Hans Biezen, Eindhoven
Domenico Capone, Rome
Roberto Cavanna, Rome
George Daffin Cope, Boston
Bevan Davies, New York
Alfio Di Bella, Rome
Dorothee Fischer, Düsseldorf
Marcello Gianvenuti, Rome
Riccardo Grassetti, Rome
Alberto Grifi, Rome
Laura Grisi, Rome
Shunk Kender, New York
Nanda Lanfranco, Genoa
Ugo Mulas, Milan
Enzo Pirozzi, Rome
Eric Pollitzer, New York
Folco Quilici, Rome
Bruno Vespasiani, Rome
Dorothy Zeidman, New York